Praise for *Here's the Story . . .*

"These stories encompass a wide range of lifetime experiences, from childhood memories to adult challenges to literary pursuits to coping with the pandemic. Each story in this collection is told with a refreshing blend of honesty and openness, infused with the author's authentic voice. By delving into their personal challenges, the authors not only invite readers to empathize with their struggles but also encourage them to view their own trials from a fresh perspective. The power of storytelling as a form of healing resonates throughout this heartfelt volume, offering a soothing balm to readers. I highly recommend finding a comfortable spot, putting up your feet, and delving into this eye-opening and powerful collection. These stories provide firsthand insight into the personal growth that can be achieved when taking the risk to share and connect with others through writing." — Helen (Len) Leatherwood, president and online class coordinator, Story Circle Network

"*Here's the Story . . . Nine Women Write Their Lives* is a charming and heartfelt collection of essays, stories, and poems by and about women. The narratives engage the reader on a wide variety of issues yet often come back to themes central to the lived female experience: girlhood memories, struggles with our mothers, the passions that enlist and enliven our imaginations, how we survived the pandemic. Each piece of writing represents a labor of love shared by the contributing authors and sets the reader on a soul-searching path of self-reflection and self-discovery. This is a highly enjoyable and thought-provoking read that celebrates the female experience even amidst stories of pain, loss, and heartbreak." — Mary Caputi, Ph.D., feminist, professor, and author of *Feminism and Power: The Need for Critical Theory*

"*Here's the Story* is an absolute pleasure to read. This extraordinary essay collection from a remarkable group of writers takes on all aspects of life, the good and bad, mothers included." — D.Z. Stone, author of *No Past Tense: Love and Survival in the Shadow of the Holocaust* and *A Fairy Tale Unmasked: The Teacher and the Nazi Slaves*

"Originating in a class called "Writing about Your Mom without Guilt," the stories, essays, and poems in this anthology range far beyond the mother-daughter dynamic. Surprising, provocative, exciting, this collection brings together a group of writers whose wisdom shines through. Whether describing Covid-era lockdowns, childhood friendships, or the art of writing, the nine authors' work will draw you in, envelop you, and make you want to keep reading until the end." — Deborah Kalb, writer, editor, book blogger, and author of the novel *Off to Join the Circus*

"So many of our lives and our families' experiences are unknown and untold. Read this wonderful collection of voices, then ask yourself what stories you, too, haven't told yet. We all need this kind of inspiration." — Ruth Pennebaker, essayist, public radio commentator, and author of the novel *Women on the Verge of a Nervous Breakthrough*

"*Here's the Story . . . Nine Women Write Their Lives* was just the tonic I needed! Reading the stories and poetry that shared the lives and seminal moments of this group of women was very much like having deep, funny, and heartbreaking conversations with people who become your friends the more you read. This wonderful collection provided valuable insight into women's lives and prompted reflection and the emergence of long-buried memories and stories of my own. This book is a treasure." — Lene Andersen, health and disability advocate, and author of *Your Life with Rheumatoid Arthritis: Tools for Managing Treatment, Side Effects and Pain*

Here's the Story . . .

Jane Mylum Gardner

Karen Finch

Linda Aronovsky Cox

Here's the Story . . .

Andrea Simon

edited by
Andrea Simon

Kathleen M. Rodgers

Stephanie Cowell

Nine Women Write Their Lives

Amy Baruch

Katherine Kirkpatrick

Rhonda Hunt-Del Bene

Bink *Bink Books*
Bedazzled Ink Publishing Company • Fairfield, California

978-1-960373-43-4 paperback

Cover Design
by

Sapling
Studio

Bink Books
a division of
Bedazzled Ink Publishing
Fairfield, California
http://www.bedazzledink.com

To all women who have a story to tell.

CONTENTS

LITERARY LIFE

SINGULAR PASSIONS

PEOPLE AND PLACES

PANDEMIC LIFE

MORE ABOUT US

or not—remain a driving force and often creep into our writing. Our mother's voice hovers over us, criticizing our words, editing our sentences, and threatening us with nothing short of banishment. As author Erica Jong said: "What use are all the struggles of your mother, your grandmother, your great-grandmother? Make no mistake, these ancestors are watching you. If you disappoint them, you disappoint yourself."

Our Online Group

In the fall of 2020, I posted a Story Circle Network (SCN) online course called "Writing about Your Mom without Guilt," an offshoot from the Texas workshop. Within days, registration reached the maximum number of eight students. Helen (Len) Leatherwood, president and online classes coordinator, said, "Who knew there were so many women wanting to write about their moms?"

Three enrollees (from Washington state, New York, and North Carolina) were members of my long-term writing group. A Texas author attended my workshop at the SCN conference. One registrant was my younger cousin from Idaho, a physician who loved to write. Three women were not personally connected: a retired commercial real estate developer from California, currently studying Italian at an American university, as well as abroad; the daughter of a Holocaust survivor, a retired communication professional from Texas, and now an entrepreneur of used books; and an artist and ghostwriter from Melbourne, Australia. We scheduled our meetings when some were finishing lunch, others dinner, and our Aussie contributor was having breakfast the following day.

After an introductory Zoom meeting, we went around the "room" voicing our expectations, focusing on our mother/daughter relationships. Within an hour, many fought back tears (and others let them flow) as we confessed long-held issues to some who were complete strangers. In our safe place, we had an immediate sense of belonging. And, since we had been sequestered because of the pandemic, we were hungry for connection.

In the following weeks, the women produced heartfelt stories. A successful writer of published historical fiction wrote about her painful childhood for the first time. A retired art teacher revealed her memories of the Ku Klux Klan. Several wrote about the death or illness of their mothers; and some experimented with the "mother in autobiography" prompt, walking in her shoes. It was not all about guilt and bitterness;

many gained new insights and appreciation of their mother's gifts, along with a newfound respect and compassion. Life experiences sometimes exposed unexpressed heartaches and regrets. Our trust in each other was unbounded; no topic was off limits.

As our last session drew to a close, we were devastated. We didn't want to leave each other. The group decided to continue monthly. We'd put the subject of our mothers aside and share other writings.

The Birth of Lady Bunch

On December 17, 2020, we met for the first time as a voluntary non-affiliated group. Counting me as the former instructor, we were nine women. We agreed on the new format. A different member would lead each monthly meeting. Beforehand, she'd email prompts or ideas for her upcoming meeting. That moderator would conduct the meeting as she saw fit. Each member could also write or speak on any subject during her allotted time.

So far, we have discussed and written about childhood trauma, travels, illnesses, reaching life's goals, friendships, colorful relatives, books, and the pandemic. Suffering a disproportionate number of major illnesses, we count ourselves as survivors extraordinaire. We have experienced "aha" moments in surprising subjects, such as our hair. And there were always tons of funny stories, complete with foreign accents and mouth-watering recipes.

Over a year later, after listening to a compelling reading, one of us flippantly suggested that we should include our best stories in an anthology. This "joke" slowly turned into reality as we searched our files. We also made suggestions about creating new stories, especially those about significant chapters in our lives. All these stories, and subsequent revisions, arrived in my inbox. After proofreading and editing, I sent them to Jane Gardner, whose eagle eyes spotted typos and inconsistencies. When the "book" coalesced, everyone became an editor. So, the process continued, and *Here's the Story . . .* was born, forty-two essays, stories, and poems.

In analyzing the contents of this book, we realized that we hadn't focused on the usual "female" subjects, such as our significant others, children, and jobs (corporate and otherwise). This was not deliberate avoidance; we veered toward what we most wanted to explore. Invariably, we wrote about the women we had been and the women we wanted to be.

Each of us had lived a full and singular life, from growing up in the Deep South to the outback in Australia to the alleys of Brooklyn to the multiple displacements as a military brat schooled in Europe. Coincidentally, we all have multiple creative talents, including painting and drawing, photography, cooking, and playing musical instruments. These interests often weave into our written pieces. Given what brought us together, we have spotlighted our moms, who often appear in seemingly unrelated stories.

As members, we believe that women are capable of generous and congenial support. We don't see a jealous bone. We lift each other during life's trials and rejoice in our successes. We are a mix of seasoned writers with several published works and those who write journals and other personal reflections. In our special place, we Lady Bunchers are equal, equal to being ourselves with something worthwhile to share. We hope you enjoy reading this sampling of our writings. As the Brady Bunch song begins, "Here's the story . . ."

— Andrea Simon, 2022

GROWING UP

THE FIRST SUNDAY IN JULY

by Jane Mylum Gardner

THE DRIVE AROUND curving country roads always takes forever when we're headed to the family reunion. Pop drives with a steady hand and whistles.

I can hardly wait to see my two older cousins, Carol, who must be twelve by now, and nine-year-old Elizabeth, who is six months older than I am. Today I have my grandparents all to myself. I secretly worry. No one at the family reunion will even notice me.

I know we are almost there when we get to the train tracks. A black-and-gold wooden sign spells out the word "Ringgold." The gray station house is overgrown with vines that blossom orange. As we bounce across the railroad track, the car slows.

Tall stalks of corn gracefully sway one way and then another. There is nothing but green and red for miles around. Green corn and green tobacco grow out of red clay dirt. Barns are here and there. Like mirrors, their tin roofs sparkle in the sun. The car slows again as rocks bounce and red dust fills the air. We close the windows in a hurry.

"Hugh's crops look mighty fine," Pop notices. His brother is a farmer. I want Pop to hurry along, but he can't. The road is too narrow, and it isn't paved. Pop comes from a big family, two brothers and a bunch of red-headed sisters. I get all confused because Pop calls each one "Sister." The whole family will be there, all the way from Kentucky to Texas, to hear Uncle Brantley preach on the first Sunday in July.

"I'm hungry," I say to Grandmother as Pop parks the car under the shady oak tree in front of the church.

"We can't eat until after church," Grandmother warns as we head quickly toward the wooden door that creaks open.

"Well, Good Lord, look who's here! Come right on in." Pop's sister grabs my hand and walks us straight down the red-carpeted aisle. "We've been waiting for y'all to get here. Church is just about to start!"

My older cousins Carol and Elizabeth scoot over, making room for me on the hard wooden pew next to them. They smile big and I see Carol wears lipstick! I look around the room at the ladies gently waving handheld cardboard fans back and forth. At the front of the church, the whirl of rotating floor fans feels good as I fight to keep my eyes open in the heat.

AFTER THE SINGING, praying, and preaching, we get back in the car and drive to Great Uncle Hugh's house, where a hundred friends and relatives have gathered. Under the shade of tall oaks, my red-haired great aunts guard the mountains of covered food on long picnic tables.

My stomach growls out loud just as my tiny Aunt Eva taps me on the shoulder. "It just warms my heart to see you again," she whispers. I melt inside. Aunt Eva's face is easy to remember and so is her tiny little voice.

My grandmother says, "Aunt Eva's face is so white, it looks like she fell into a bag of flour." But I am not allowed to ask!

As the elderly sisters swat the flies away and the hands of hungry children, Aunt Esther leans toward me. "Well, I know you must be hungry after such a long trip."

"Yes, Sister, I'm starving." I looked into kind blue eyes and then stared at a big pink mole on her nose, which helps me remember her better.

"Here," she says, pressing a soft ham biscuit and a napkin into my hand, "but don't tell anybody!" She winks.

I look for my favorite dessert, the tall fluffy white coconut cake Aunt Carter bakes every year. When I finally spot it, one slice is missing. Somebody has sneaked a piece! I must be the first in line, so I won't miss out on that cake. Close by, Pop's baby brother, Uncle Hugh, dips out a cup of ice-cold lemonade from a wooden keg and places it in my hand. His smiling blue eyes are on me. But I know coconut cake is his favorite, too.

We finally gather in a large circle as quiet settles over our family. Great Uncle Brantley then bows his head and puts his hands on my shoulders, praying. "Dear Heavenly Father, I give thanks for my parents, for my brothers and sisters and for all their children. We thank you for our friends and everyone here today. And we thank you especially for this fine food, Amen." Uncle Brantley's voice is strong and sweet. I know he means every single word he says as he squeezes my shoulders.

This is the only quiet moment. The smell of cows and pigs floats in the breeze. I breathe in deep, loving that smell just as a short woman walks up and stands close to my face. "I have been looking for you!" she says, squinting to see me through thick eyeglasses.

Recognizing her strange Virginia accent, I squeal "Aunt Kathleen!" She has the most unusual way of rolling words around in her mouth. As we hug, I notice I am almost as tall as her.

"Here," she says proudly as she hands me a big jar of my favorite plum preserves. "I made this just for you. I know how much you enjoyed the last jar I gave you! I will ask your grandmother to put it in a safe place!"

Before I can even say thank you, Uncle Hugh interrupts us.

"Well, Sis, I'm telling you, there's no finer food in the state of Virginia. Now let's go eat!"

Since Aunt Kathleen is almost blind, Uncle Hugh gently guides her arm as we walk down the food line. Behind them, I fill my plate and then get another one, just for dessert.

"This is about as close to heaven as a hungry man can get," Uncle Hugh says, and I agree with him.

When we finally get to the coconut cake, I carefully place the very last slice on my dessert plate. How lucky I am!

"Here, let me give you a hand," Uncle Hugh says as he helps me put down both plates. "It's so nice of you to get your old uncle Hugh a piece of his favorite coconut cake." He chuckles as he wiggles his ears at me.

I gulp! "But it's my favorite cake, too."

"Yes, I remember," he says. "Well, I'll be more than happy to give you the first bite!"

I turn red, not knowing if he is joking with me or not.

"You know, by the looks of your plate, I imagine you'll be back here again next year."

"Yes, sir, I imagine you're right!" I say to Uncle Hugh as I lick my greasy fingers. Each bite of chicken and potato salad tastes better than the last. After I clean my plate, I wash it down with the cold lemonade. Uncle Hugh hands me a fork, and I take a big bite of the everlasting wonderful coconut cake. I close my eyes. The icing melts on my tongue and all the way down to the tips of my toes.

When I open my eyes, Uncle Hugh beams and takes a great big spoonful of my cake. "Let me taste that cake to see if it's any good or not," he says. "Well, I guess it's all right, but I need just one more bite to make sure!"

As I watch him take another big spoonful of my coconut cake, I don't know what to say. He wiggles his ears at me again! And then we both laugh.

"Watch out for Uncle Hugh! He is full of pranks and always has been!" Pop had warned me.

Excused from the table, I run off to find my cousins. We kick rocks down the hill, careful not to disturb the cows crunching long strands of grass in the field. Standing beside the black iron fence at the little graveyard, Carol unlatches the gate to the final resting place of our great grandparents, Jasper and Kat.

"Mama says after they died, Uncle Hugh started the family reunions," Carol says. "He thinks everyone needs to come home at least once a year!"

Sweaty, Carol latches the graveyard gate, and we take off running down the dusty red path that leads past the apple tree.

Beyond the graveyard stands the tall white house Jasper built. All of Kat's children, Uncle Hugh, Uncle Brantley, even Pop and their five sisters, were born in this old house. These are the fields they worked and grew their food. Pop even brought Grandmother to live here on their wedding day. Now Carol lives in the same old house, which is bigger and much prettier than the crowded house where I live.

Next to the side of the house, the garden hose lies on the ground. "Just take off your sandals," Carol orders as she sprays Elizabeth and me down, shorts and all.

But the red clay caked to the hose gets all over me. "Grandmother's going to kill us if you don't get this red clay off me!" I scream. And then I grab the hose and spray them both down.

As the three of us lay in the grass, my wet clothes feel cool. Carol shows us how to put on lipstick. I am afraid to try it, but she is bossy. Carol combs my straight hair and Elizabeth's curls.

"I can't believe I got freckles and the two of you don't have any at all," Carol complains.

"Well, one day, we might have red-headed kids with freckles just like you," Elizabeth says.

"That would be just fine with me," I say while I pick out a tiny rock caught in my sandal.

"You know, everyone in the family got their red hair and freckles from Kat and Jasper," Carol explains.

We play a card game on the grass and then meander beyond the house, down a dirt path to the barns under the shade of old pecan trees. The minutes evaporate like the heat. We turn back around after we look at the old red tractor that Carol knows how to drive.

"I think we should go back to Uncle Hugh's house," I say, worried. We hadn't kept track of time, but at least the afternoon sun had dried our clothes.

"Can't you stay here with us for a few days?" Elizabeth begs. "We can give you some clothes to wear and a toothbrush," she promises as we trudge back up to the house on top of the hill.

But I know the answer. Pop wants to be home by dark, and he won't change his mind. "Maybe next year," I say as tears run down my face. "I want to stay more than anything!"

Just before we pull away, Uncle Hugh leans over the car window for a final goodbye. I can't look at him, afraid I'll cry even more.

"Now don't forget me," Uncle Hugh says. "Your grandpa's promised to bring you back here soon as he can. I'll take you fishing! And by the way, here's a little something Aunt Carter and I want you to have in case you get hungry on your way home."

He hands me the brown paper bag, then pats my cheek with his rough farmer's hands. I look at him and whisper, "Thank you, Uncle Hugh." I turn away. Out the back window, Carol and Elizabeth wait for me to wave goodbye.

As Pop drives on slowly down that bumpy road, I look back again. But all I see is red dust. Far behind us, rocks kick up. After a long while, I peek inside the bag. There is a napkin and wrapped in wax paper is the finest piece of coconut cake you ever did lay your eyes on.

"What?" I blurt.

Then, it hits me. "So that's what happened to the missing piece of cake!" I announce to my grandparents in the front seat of the car, as I taste salty tears.

I eat slowly. The cake melts in my mouth.

"We always go back home with much more than we've taken," Pop says.

"I know." I smile, licking the crumbs of cake off the wax paper as Pop drives with a steady hand and whistles all the way back home.

SUPER TRIPLETS FOR LIFE

by Andrea Simon

I HAVE OFTEN written about identical twins. In my novel *Esfir Is Alive*, there were mirror twins, the loyal Liba and Fanny, in Aunt Perl's boardinghouse; and twins appeared in a children's picture book I drew in a black leather-bound book when I was a girl. I wrote versions of my semi-autobiographical novel nearly thirty years ago; and in each, the protagonist spent her childhood playing with identical twins. For a while, the title was the very uncreative, *Best Friends*. By the time this morphed into *Floating in the Neversink*, I killed off one sister in fear of being labeled "the twin stalker." The newly amalgamated character's name was Francine. To distinguish her from my former twin embodiments, Francine was whiny, afraid to jump over boulders, and mired in hay fever. I workshopped her stories in my MFA courses. My fellow students coined a word in their critical repertoire for any wimpy character, often asking their classmates, "Are you Francining her?"

All these girl portrayals were based on their real-life counterparts: identical twins, Joanie and Carol, my best friends from the age of four for me and three for them, when I lived on a tenement dead-end enclave in Brooklyn's Flatbush section until 1960. At fourteen, my family moved to the snooty Midwood area, and I had to make new friends with girls who had teased beehives and wore circle pins on their lapels. But before this heartache, I spent the best ten years of my life in the middle, surrounded by curly-brown-haired, freckle-faced Joanie and Carol. Neighbors often stopped them on the street, asked their names, and said to each, "Are you sure you're Joanie?" or "Are you sure you're Carol?" Joanie, the oldest by six minutes, was most sure and said yes, while Carol looked at Joanie and then nodded. I often wondered what such questions could do to their self-images.

But as far as I was concerned, I longed to merge my identity. I pulled my long, straight hair into a similar ponytail and hoped by walking in the middle I would obscure my smaller facial features. Dressed alike in white angora hats with towels safety-pinned to the back of our blue parkas, we trolled our streets like rodents with chalk sticks to mark our secret paths. We became the Super Triplets of Flatbush.

I already wrote about Francine (in reality, Carol) and I making stinky ice cream from hard-boiled eggs, of how the Super Triplets stole hard suckers from the outside bins of the candy store while the owner chased us down the street threatening to put us in jail. I described how the twins and I played Sorry! for hours and made crank calls to people in the Brooklyn phone book named Marx and asked to speak to "Groucho." I reconstructed our lunches at the Golden Star Chinese Restaurant as we indulged in lobster Cantonese, followed by fortune cookies, which we saved in our wallets flattened behind a lone dollar bill.

Sadly, I portrayed the terror I experienced each summer as I left for the Catskill Mountains and "Francine," aka the twins, stayed behind to swim at Brighton Beach's private pool club and the Catholic girls pressured them to switch allegiances. For two hot months, I sweated over my Labor Day return and the twins possibly shunning me.

Did I write about sleeping over at the twins' house with my pillow and *Gone with the Wind* Melanie doll when we whispered and giggled all night, and how I threatened to bite Carol's toes when she fell asleep? Joanie always protected her "younger" sister, but was happy to conspire with me and untuck the covers from Carol's feet.

I WAS IMPRESSED with the twins' parents, who had a relationship more like the Andersons in *Father Knows Best* than my parents, the Simons, on East 22nd Street. Their parents, to my amazement, went to restaurants for dinner. And their mother, Roz, had a red-and-white Betty Crocker cookbook, from which she concocted imaginative recipes like tuna casserole. Could that have been the time my mother called Roz to get the recipe for the spaghetti dish I always raved about? "Oh," Roz had said to my mother, "I use butter and ketchup."

As Super Triplets, we roamed around the metal garbage-can alleyways and iron-barred back windows behind the liquor and hardware stores on Flatbush Avenue that abutted our dead-end street, often chased by boys in Lone Ranger masks flinging chalk-filled socks. We rounded up criminals, slid down metal basement covers to evade the worst of the lot, and locked up the bad guys in the pretend jail, the iron-barred windows of Ralph's grocery store. But the best times for me were huddling in a secluded corner in the back area of our joined apartment buildings. There we played our favorite game of Family, whose scenarios I often made up on the spot. The plot often found the baby, always my role, in danger—kidnapping, animal attack, or plain parental abuse—and Joanie as the baby's mother and Carol as the aunt enclosed their pudgy arms around me, the weeping baby. Nobody allowed me to enact my "stories" and soothe my anxieties like the twins.

FAST-FORWARD SIXTY years and we remain bound to each other by more than our capes. Even though Joanie lives in Florida and Carol on Long Island, we'd get together a few times a year before the pandemic. We called these reunions our Super Triplet weekend, and we celebrated with our three identical four-inch dolls. Like us, we could always tell them apart. Joanie's has a multicolored beaded necklace; Carol's a hairband; and mine is missing a leg and her hair is sticking out like a witch. The last time we were together at a hotel in Florida, we put the miniature girls on the windowsill facing the pool and slid them across the ledge as they giggled and whooped just like their human mothers, the Super Triplets of Flatbush.

Ballet recital, about 1955. *Left to right:* Carol, Andrea, Joanie.

We look pretty good as seniors. *Left to right:* Carol, Andrea, and Joanie.

FIREFLIES ON KENAN STREET

by Jane Mylum Gardner

THE ONLY THING I hated about my grandparents' house was tiptoeing over creepy big black water bugs that crawled across the bathroom floor at night. While I was still an only child, Mama, Daddy, and I lived in the two-story gray house that Pop and Grandmother rented for over forty years. They raised their two sons there, and it was Daddy's house when he was a kid.

I was the first grandchild born and the joy my paternal grandmother had longed for after her two infant daughters died shortly after birth. I was the one whose hair she combed, who accompanied her on tricycle rides to the homes of her friends between Daniel and Bruton Streets. While everyone worked during the day, I was in the quiet care of my tiny little grandmother in the old wooden house on Kenan Street.

I can recall a winter night when my short legs dangled down over Pop's lap, but my toes could not touch the floor. We always sat in the living room around the stove after dinner. Even though the heavy green window shades were pulled down to keep out the cold, they did not prevent the sound of the howling wind that jangled the windowsills. The black potbelly coal stove in the kitchen looked very different from the bigger, shiny brown one in the living room. There was fire in both, but the one in the kitchen had a teakettle full of water that puffed steam into the air. The adults didn't allow me to stand too close.

After dinner, my parents sat on the dark green couch, while my grandfather Ernest Mylum sat in his chair close to the stove in the living room. Pop fed it black chunks of coal that crackled and made the fire inside wiggle. His chair was bigger and taller than my grandmother's. As he read the newspaper out loud by a lamp that stood over his right shoulder, I climbed into his lap. The rumbling brown stove kept the room warm. But the stove was not big enough to heat the adjacent dining room, so we kept those double glass doors closed. Like the windows, the doors jiggled and danced to the sound of wind when it was blistering cold outdoors.

There was just enough room on Pop's lap for me to fit right under his arm and for the newspaper to make a circle around us. One night, Pop took a pen out of his shirt pocket, folded up the paper; and on the side of the comics page, he drew a circle, and then a stick to which he joined two stick arms and stick legs and fingers and feet. I had never seen anything like this in my life.

It was truly hard to believe, to write on a paper like this. I stared at it; no one had shown me how to draw before. He did it again, only this time Pop held my hand in his and we drew it together. Delighted with myself, I took the newspaper from his hands and showed it to my mother and father, but "uh-hum" was all the response I got. In an instant, my joy evaporated.

On one side of the living room, directly across from Pop's chair, was a tall wooden box, a radio that daily provided the adventures of Br'er Rabbit. Later some evenings, the grown-ups gathered their chairs around it and laughed uncontrollably at the different voices of Amos and Andy, Bob Hope, and Jack Benny. The box that talked was magical to me. Sometimes my mother held me in her arms as we sat back and listened to the stories coming out of it, as familiar voices became murmurs and sleep gradually carried me into a world beyond the living room. What I loved most was the sound of those voices mingling with the sputtering of the stove.

In the summer, we didn't gather in the living room much. There were three hardback wooden chairs in Pop and Grandmother's backyard, where we ate peaches or drank sweet, iced tea after supper. As the sky changed colors, stars appeared in the dark sky. The shadows and the night air were a welcome relief at the end of a hot summer's day. The ice cubes in the tea glasses melted as fireflies dotted those dark nights, when I first noticed things flying around in the air with lights on their tails. Pop gave me a glass jar to catch them.

Fireflies. Glass jars. Night sky, just me and Pop and Grandmother. Like the chirping of the crickets, I liked the twinkling sky. We listened to see if the stars or the fireflies made sounds like the crickets. But no, Pop said the stars were silent, and I was the loudest one of all God's creatures.

Pop often told stories, but the one I loved most, he told me time and time again. "When you look up at the night sky, you will always remember that God loves the stars and the moon," he said. "But I love you even more. The stars will be there to remind you in case you ever forget."

I was three years old then, and my world was so utterly perfect, so complete. I will never forget Pop's words and that night sky.

Prompt: Did you play a musical instrument as a kid? If so, did you enjoy it or hate it?

LET THE MUSIC PLAY

by Karen Finch

"MAKE SURE THE children have music," so said Aunty Marea, a courtesy title. She wasn't my aunt. She was a friend of my grandmother, who died just before I turned two. According to family lore, my grandmother was reputed to have had a fine, if untrained, voice.

We left Sydney when I was nine and a half, which coincided with Aunty Marea and Uncle Gordon selling up to travel the country in a Ford Transit van fitted as a mobile home. So, Aunty Marea's piano joined our household goods and became mine, replacing the very dodgy cheap upright.

We arrived in the small country town where my father had a job as a draftsman working on a new national railway line. Mum contacted the local convent of Saint Joseph, a teaching order that ran the Catholic primary school, to find me a piano teacher to continue the lessons that had started in Sydney before we left.

I'd never met a nun before. She was tall and thin, a column of black from the toes of her very shiny shoes, all the way up via her floor-length habit to a face contained within a white wimple, surmounted by a long black veil. A stern face that looked as if it didn't know how to smile anymore.

That face never did smile. It frowned a lot. For the first time since starting piano, I was confronted with a graded syllabus and exams. Endless scales and aural tests, exercises, and classical pieces, along with an extra weekly session learning music theory. Mistakes on the keyboard were met by the ruler's edge hitting my knuckles. Mistakes in theory meant the hard cane handle of a feather duster. Week after week of fear and abuse, I came to hate that piano. I passed my grade three exams, piano and theory, because I was terrified of what might happen if I didn't.

The theory lessons ended when I got to high school, replaced by classes there. I had a pass to ride my bike from school during lunch hour to have my piano lesson. One day, I decided not to go. It lasted for almost a term.

I didn't tell anyone, fear mounting about what Mum would say. She asked about what I was learning for the grade four exam. I mumbled something about a new book. Finally, I couldn't deal with the subterfuge and told Mum I'd not been going all term, and why.

"Why didn't you tell me?" she asked.

"I didn't know if you'd believe me," I replied.

"Why wouldn't I believe you?"

"Because she's a nun!" I said, wondering how she couldn't understand that.

Without another word, Mum dropped the topic. When I got home from school the next day, Mum was waiting for me with an opened envelope and letter. She passed it to me. It was from the nun. She'd written to tell Mum I'd not been to lessons for some time, asking whether I would continue, in which case, there were fees owing.

I started to cry. "Please don't make me go back, Mum!"

"I won't. I'm going there to tell her you won't be back, and why. I'll just have to find another teacher for you."

For a while, I learned piano from the father of a schoolmate. No exams, no real classical music either. Songs and musical theater. Mum wasn't happy about that.

However, at school, having hit second year high, I signed up for music and was assigned a clarinet. Mum thought that would be nice; I could learn to play "Strangers in the Night" like the British musician, Acker Bilk. I didn't even know who that was! I didn't like the clarinet very much.

Our school music teacher was busy forming a band—the first band in the town high school. He was young and enthusiastic, ready to build a proper music program. I remember being parked in the front row with the other clarinet students and playing my part in tunes like "When the Saints Go Marching In" and various marches.

Shivers went up and down my spine with the feel of the reed in my mouth, especially if my bottom teeth hit it. How unforgiving the instrument was in the early days, producing loud discordant squeaks instead of the dulcet tones on Mum's Acker Bilk record. I listened to a classmate who'd started clarinet at the same time. He was working his way through the slow movement of the Mozart clarinet concerto at the beginning of our second year on the instrument, while I was still playing tunes from the daily lesson book.

I restarted piano lessons back at the convent after the old nun retired, and a new, younger one took her place. She obeyed the precepts of Vatican

Two and had done away with the old black habit, clad instead in a short blue dress, with a navy veil that showed bits of her hair sticking out. With her, I made it through the grade four exam.

Back at school, I was more and more unhappy with my clarinet. Playing in the band was fun, but that was mostly because of the larger group experience. One day, I walked into the music room at the end of the school day to pick it up for band practice, and the brass teacher was there with my music teacher. He had something that looked like a baby tuba. A euphonium. I asked if I could hold it. I sat in a chair with my arms hugging it. The instrument spoke as I blew into it. Oh, I liked this!

"Can I play this, please? I really hate clarinet," I asked.

"I'm sorry, Karen," replied the music teacher. "It's been assigned already."

The brass teacher spoke up, "I have a French horn that's not being used. The department gives us all the instruments I might have to teach, and I don't have anyone learning horn. It's not doing the instrument any good, not being played. Hang on, I'll get it from the car."

He came back into the classroom, laid a weirdly shaped, bulky case on a desk, and opened it. He lifted out miles of shiny brass curled around itself and opening into a massive bell. "Here, have a go with this. It'll be more difficult than the euphonium to make a sound, as the mouthpiece is so much smaller. Just buzz into the mouthpiece first, to get a feel for it."

I buzzed. I put the mouthpiece back on the horn, took a breath, and blew. Oh, the sound. Such a glorious sound. Rich and big, and warm.

"Well done!" said the brass teacher. "Here's the lesson book. Look through it this week and have your first lesson next week."

"Oh, and Karen," said the music teacher, "you'll need to get your mother to sign this form for the instrument. You may as well stay put and play clarinet for rehearsal today, though."

I walked out of rehearsal towards Mum, who was waiting for me in the car.

"What's *that*?" she demanded, as I got in the car.

"My new French horn," I said. "I'm swapping from clarinet."

"You're what? Why?"

"Because I hate clarinet! I never wanted to play it. You wanted me to play it, and I hate it. So, the brass teacher gave me his horn."

I battled my way through the next week after school every day, coaxing notes out of that horn. They're so unforgiving for pitching. Fifteen feet of conical brass tubing, and a tiny little mouthpiece. It's so easy, I found, to aim for one note, and land on something entirely different. But I loved it!

The next week, I stepped into a new seat in the band, among the brass. I hit many wrong notes, but more right ones, and I was off. A year later, I was playing my own slow movement of a Mozart horn concerto, first as the free choice piece in a grade five exam, and then again at the end-of-year concert as a solo piece. I kept going too, and did music as a final year subject, the first graduating French horn student in the entire region.

I GOT INTO the Conservatorium at the University of Adelaide as a horn player and performed in an orchestra for the first time. I started out in the fourth horn chair. In my second year, the head of the brass school did a reshuffle, and I found myself playing first. I remember sweating my way through the first horn part of the Brahms second symphony with a visiting Israeli conductor, Eliakum Shapirra. Brahms had a best mate who was a horn player, so his orchestral music is littered with massive horn solos, and that symphony has three huge solos for the first horn. When we'd played that symphony the previous year, I was in the fourth horn chair, bumping along with a harmonizing part.

Mum was determined to see me graduate and become Australia's second Barry Tuckwell, who'd risen to international fame as a concert soloist on the French horn. It was not to be. The head of singing "discovered" me in an elective singing class one Friday morning when she was recruiting for chorus in the full-scale opera production, the first held at the Conservatorium in many years.

Despite my protests that I wasn't a singer and had already started rehearsing for the opera in the orchestra, she looked me up and down from her four feet, eleven inches to my five feet, seven inches, and stated, in her fruity, don't-mess-with-me voice, "This institution currently has five French horn students. The opera is scored for four horns. They don't need you. I do."

After the opera, Puccini's *Suor Angelica*, in which I was, ironically, a nun, she summoned me to her office. Pointing to the chair across from her desk, she told me to sit down.

"You *do* know you have a *voice*, do you not?" she asked, emphasizing "voice," although it felt more as if I was being told.

I just looked at her.

"I have arranged for you to start singing lessons. You mustn't waste it."

THOSE LESSONS WITH a senior student became lessons with a professional teacher after I dropped out of the Conservatorium and got married. When my then-husband and I relocated to Canberra, Australia's capital city, for his PhD studies, I was accepted by the city's top singing teacher on the recommendation of another student, a colleague of my husband's. My husband thought it was nonsense and wouldn't pay for lessons, so I sold my French horn. The teacher sent me to a local community college to learn Italian after she informed me I would sing opera while playing me a recording of Joan Sutherland singing the title role of *Lucia di Lammermoor*. However, I lacked those top notes and the agility of a dramatic *coloratura* soprano. She insisted I take a grade-five singing exam, despite my protests, but she had already enrolled me.

The results of that exam coincided with the arrival of the semester results of the Italian exam. I got a high distinction for the singing, and a distinction for Italian, and raced off to the university to tell my husband. He was most displeased that I'd interrupted his work in the middle of the day, although his singer friend was delighted for me. Later that evening, I said I wanted to enroll in an arts degree to study languages for opera. His response was to query who would then iron his shirts and look after our son. Then he said the most hurtful thing. "You just don't have the talent!"

That was the beginning of the end of a marriage that already had serious cracks. Ultimately, I packed up my son, and we returned to Adelaide, where I re-enrolled at the Conservatorium once we were settled into suitable housing. I got my first solo opera role the following year in the Conservatorium production of Malcolm Williamson's *The Happy Prince*. It was a pants role, a mezzo-soprano playing a male character, The Author. My tall, slim frame was costumed convincingly as a man, and it opened a whole new world of possible roles.

The following year, I auditioned successfully for the State Opera Company of South Australia as a chorister and was contracted as part of the Ethiopian chorus in a massive production of Verdi's *Aida,* marking what would become fifteen years as a professional opera singer. By then, my voice had settled, and I was a true alto with a solid bottom range, which made me valuable for an opera company. I did most of the productions over that time in the chorus, but also had extra contracts as a cover for principals, minor principal roles, and separate acting roles.

Since the city was small, and opera was a very niche form of the arts in Australia, the company was essentially part time, so my professional life encompassed those chorus contracts and freelance singing in a variety of musical forms. The jobs included singing jazz classics in a big band and becoming part of a small period trio, specializing in the standards from the thirties, forties, and fifties. I also had solo gigs with different bands, including singing carols by candlelight, in front of audiences of fifteen thousand people.

Then another interstate move happened after the death of my mother, who had never come to grips with her daughter, the opera singer. The cantor of a synagogue in Sydney headhunted me to become a member of the only professional Jewish choir in the country, and I spent four years as a member of the ensemble and a cantorial soloist. I also performed with other professional choirs in the city that included symphonic choral works and recorded movie soundtracks.

I felt the most enormous surge of achievement well up inside me the first time I left the world-renown Sydney Opera House after a rehearsal for an upcoming concert there and walked through the many people wandering the concourse at Circular Quay, taking photos with the House in the background. I had just been singing on the stage of this famous concert hall—and was being paid to be there. It reminded me of receiving my first paycheck for *Aida*, and realizing that despite all the naysayers, I really *could* sing, and had the type of voice that could offer me a career.

These days, making music isn't part of my creative output. The lifelong juggle of music, fine art, and writing has collided with circumstances beyond my control—the COVID pandemic—and now art and writing are uppermost. But I'll always be a singer.

Manon Lescaut, 1997. Karen is standing, second row, far right.

Cavalleria Rusticana, 2003. Karen wears black dress, front, right.

YOU GOTTA HAVE FRIENDS

by Linda Aronosky Cox

Military families move—a lot. As the child of an Air Force officer, I grew up in seven homes, four cities, and three states. The isolation from my extended family felt profound, and the short sojourns hindered developing deep relationships with others. As a highly sensitive child of an alcoholic father and overwhelmed mother, with four siblings, I was forced to rely almost exclusively on my family in lieu of other supportive adults, though this was grievously inadequate. When my life in a loud, chaotic, abusive home became too oppressive, the pain and trauma too intense, the only way to escape was with friends. Here is the story of a special one.

THE EARLY 1970s was a dizzying time to be a teenager living in Europe. The Vietnam War was at its height, and the stateside protests were feverishly heating. In Europe, the anti-American sentiments were strong, but the hippie movement promoting peace and free love and lots of drugs, especially hashish and hallucinogens, was in full force. I loved being in the middle of it all.

My family had just moved to Madrid from Wiesbaden, Germany, in December 1970, for my father's reassignment—to our eleventh home, seventh city, and fourth country. It represented our sixth major relocation and would turn out to be our last as a military family. I was midway through my junior year of high school. This was to be my third high school, with my freshman year in Montreal, Canada, where we had moved to be with my mother's family while my father served in Vietnam, followed by Germany.

As an experienced military brat (a term I loathe), I knew it wouldn't be too difficult to meet new friends in the school on the military base in Madrid, even mid-school year, since we were all short-term residents, two to three years at most, and there was no time to dilly-dally about. Unlike typical public schools, there were no cliques or judgmental biases, because no one had known each other for long. We got close and formed free-flowing groups, and we did it swiftly and easily.

With little effort, I found my group, the friends who would make up my world for the one and a half years left in my high school life, some of whom would remain my friends. And shining through them all was my best friend, Angelina. She was as tall as I was short (six feet vs. five feet, two inches), light as I was dark (vivid blond hair vs. dark brown), slim as I was plump. The contrast was so striking that we heard that someone had painted our portrait while we walked through a field.

Not only was Angelina my buddy and my drug partner, but she was also an escape from my hellish family life. By then, my father's alcoholism and abuse had progressed to an impossibly unbearable home environment. Angelina's elegant, expansive home was my haven. It was the epitome of everything mine wasn't—calm, quiet, and serene. Her father was an embassy attaché, and they lived in the heart of Madrid. The upper floor was reserved for Angelina and her three siblings; each private bedroom had its own bathroom and balcony (perfect for our daily hashish smoking), all surrounding a large central living area. Her parents never came upstairs, and we only ventured down to get food, to play cards with her mother (once after dropping acid while waiting for the trip to begin!), or to leave. I spent nearly all my free time there.

We finished our junior year and looked ahead to three months before the start of our senior year. American kids could not work in Spain, and teenagers could not drive until they were eighteen. There was no American television, no scheduled activities. But of course, we could do what our group usually did on weekends—with no minimum drinking age, we could have fun at the bars in downtown Madrid, explore the city, appreciate the arts at the Prado, hike to a nearby mesa with exploratory hallucinogens, or go to the American movie theater to see the at-least-year-old movies showing there. It was a safe time for us American teenagers to carouse around Madrid at all hours—the dictator *Generalissimo* Franco was in power, and his private force, *la Guardia Civil,* would not tolerate any crime, especially against Americans, so we could hitchhike or travel by bus, day or night, and feel safe. And despite the danger of getting caught by the police or by our parents, we smoked hashish nearly all the time.

Angelina and I were suddenly taken with the idea of leaving Madrid that summer and going on a trip around Europe. Just the two of us!

The only obstacle was our parents' permission. That summer, Angelina was barely seventeen, and I was only sixteen. Somehow, I talked my mother into it. I don't remember my father being cognizant enough to even voice an opinion, and my mother was preoccupied with him and raising my three younger siblings. But Angelina's parents were another matter. They were normal, caring, concerned parents, and it took a lot of reasoning, begging, and reassurance to convince them to allow us to go. There were several restrictions and requirements, including being back by a certain date.

Admittedly, it was a bit safer for us because of the passports we carried. Angelina had the black one issued to diplomats' families, and I had the green one issued to Americans living abroad. We purchased our rucksacks, not the fancy backpacks with frames that the American kids wore. We were proudly almost European! We packed just two changes of clothes, put two hundred dollars in our woven Greek shoulder bags, and carried a bottle of Evian water that we refilled wherever we could find potable water.

So off we went, joining the hordes of American kids that summer traveling Europe on student-rail passes that covered two months of travel for $125. These were the days of *Europe on $5 a Day*, but my book of choice was *Vagabonding in Europe and North Africa,* which promised, "How to visit Europe as a way of blowing your mind." First printing, July 1971.

We were adventurous, following wherever our interests and hearts led us, and mostly deciding from one day to the next where we wanted to go. We visited Basque territory in northern Spain, Arles in the south of France, Nice on the French Riviera, and Paris at the beautiful estate of Angelina's longtime family friends where she had lived for many years while her father was at the American embassy. Angelina was fluent in French and that reinvigorated my love of the language, which I originally learned in school when we lived in Montreal. We were, ah, so sophisticated, so continental, so young, *très extraordinaire*!

After France, we headed east for a somber visit to Dachau, the concentration camp in Germany, in honor of my mother, who had escaped Belgium during the Holocaust. Angelina later told me she was forever changed after seeing it.

On to the hashish haven of Amsterdam, then Copenhagen, and finally Bern in the Alps of Switzerland. Throughout our travels, we lived on hunks of cheese, olives, fruit, and fresh bread that we purchased at the local market; no bourgeois restaurants for us. We stayed in local youth hostels, meeting teens from around the world, and rejoiced in our shared freedom and ability to communicate despite our myriad languages.

We had been traveling more than two weeks and planned on longer, but Angelina suddenly had to go home, for a family-related reason that now escapes me. She knew that once we returned, her mother would not allow her to leave again, even though we had not yet visited everywhere we wanted. As she predicted, that was the end of our travels together. I continued to travel alone that summer, and the following summer after I graduated, friends and I visited Morocco and overland in Europe to Greece.

And then it was over. In late summer of 1972, my family moved back to the United States, my parents separated (and ultimately divorced), and I went off to begin college in Ohio, living independently from that point forward.

Despite my difficult childhood, during what were arguably my most formative years, ages thirteen to eighteen, I looked outwardly and matured, learning how to be a sensitive and aware adult. I lived internationally in three different countries. I learned to speak French in school and passable Spanish on the street, appreciated classic art and the finest museums, embraced other cultures and peoples of all kinds, valued compassion and kindness, and spurned the superficiality and materialism of most Americans. I was confident and secure and unafraid of venturing out on my own.

Postscript

Forty years ago, I moved to Austin, Texas, setting down roots and managing decades-long friendships that sustain me.

WHEN THE KKK RODE THROUGH TOWN

by Jane Mylum Gardner

THE VIETNAM WAR and civil rights were two issues that could have easily gotten me kicked out of the house or even killed in the 1960s. White Southern girls like me just didn't discuss these ills—they were swept under the rug and better left unspoken.

Though I had never gone to school with Black students, this changed in the fall of 1965 during my sophomore year in college. Four Black females and four Black males were admitted to my state-supported, soon-to-be-university, East Carolina College in Greenville, North Carolina. Two of the females moved into our all-girl's dorm, across the hall from me. Shirley and her roommate, Carol, a wild one who preferred to be called by her last name, "Battle," were as different as Mutt and Jeff from the comic strip.

Shirley, a dress size fourteen, wore her almost shoulder-length hair slicked back in a ponytail or curled softly in a more traditional style. She was quiet, careful not to step on anyone's toes, kept an immaculate room, and read her Bible daily. Her roommate Battle, on the other hand, entered the dorm dancing down the hallway, listening to an entirely different drummer. Battle apparently wanted to party at college, not to study. Skinny as a rail, she sported a bold Afro. Shirley quickly adapted and stepped out of Carol Battle's way.

Shirley arrived at college proudly showing off her boyfriend's huge senior high-school class ring, which weighed her hand down but served as a symbol of their serious relationship. They wrote letters to each other constantly since the pay telephone in the booth at the end of the hallway was shared and kept busy by forty-three other teenage girls.

Shirley and I were a lot alike. We wore similar clothes: conservative blouses with Peter Pan collars and matching sweater sets with plaid or plain skirts. We slowly got to know each other.

IN THE SUMMER of 1964, a few White Northerners, college students, arrived to paint Shirley's church in Elm City, a small farming community about sixty miles east of Raleigh and about nine miles northeast of Wilson, my hometown.

"Didn't you read about it in the newspaper or see the news on TV?" Shirley asked me one evening over dinner in the student cafeteria.

"Well, sorta, I heard about it." I didn't tell her that I couldn't imagine such an incident happening so close to home.

Shirley continued, almost whispering, as she checked to see if anyone could hear our conversation. "The parsonage, my home, is next door to the church."

Slowly, it dawned on me. Shirley was there!

"We woke up in the middle of the night and looked out the window. Men were waving torches in the dark. There was a strong smell of gasoline. They were standing so close to our house. I was absolutely terrified. I'll never forget it."

"Go on," I said, my heart pounding from the image.

"I was afraid they'd light a match to the church or to our house. The men were swearing, and then there were gunshots in the air. We had nowhere to run!"

"Was it the Klan?" I asked.

"No, it wasn't the Klan. No white sheets, no pointed hats, just plain White folks."

"So, what did they do?"

"Preacher man," one hollered to my daddy, who stood at the front door in his bathrobe. "Get those damn White Yankees out of this town! They got no business being here. If you think you see trouble now, you ain't seen nothing yet!"

The members of the volunteer fire department arrived as the men disappeared into the dark woods, down a country road, Shirley explained, adding, "thankfully before the church caught on fire."

I pictured this scene and looked her in the eye. Appropriate words couldn't come. Of course, she noticed the horrified expression on my face and understood that I was empathic to her nightmare. Finally, I said, "I am glad the church didn't burn down."

Clearly, the threat of a cross burning or a church going up in flames was enough trouble for a one-stoplight town with one filling station and a population of less than eight hundred. Shirley was still shaken by the retelling. She said, "I never feel completely safe when I go into town now. I always wonder who is watching me."

I tried to understand her terror, but I couldn't.

SHIRLEY'S HOME WAS thirty minutes out of my way. I had a car, a means to get home to Wilson on weekends, but she didn't, being a freshman. So, it seemed natural that I should offer her a ride home.

When Daddy asked why I arrived home later than usual, I told him, "I gave a friend a ride home from school this afternoon." I didn't describe her race, but somehow he knew.

"Well," he warned, "if you want to keep that car, I better not hear about you ever giving that n-girl in your dorm a ride." The discussion was finished. "Our house will become a target! Do you understand me?"

His face turned redder by the minute, his fists and jaws clenched. I was in trouble.

"Is that what you want?" he asked me. I didn't answer him. As usual, he had been drinking.

"Did anyone see you dropping that girl off in her driveway?" he raised his voice with urgency.

"I don't think so."

ONLY A FEW weeks later that fall, the KKK, wearing their white sheets, rode their horses right through the streets of Wilson as part of the homecoming parade. I couldn't see their faces, only their darting eyes through the holes in their masks, and the black polished rifles cradled in their arms. I heard their silent threats as they kicked the sides of their snorting horses with their spurred boots. They were ten feet away, as I stood petrified behind the barriers that roped off the crowd from the street.

These were just plain ole hometown folks, a secret society of men holding on to the past of the Civil War, full of community pride. Just as ordinary as white bread and mayonnaise sandwiches, a serving of White ONLY matters community pride.

Later at home, no one spoke about this part of the parade. But within weeks, there was another incident. Bill Bussey, our minister, announced four days in advance that a Black minister would lead the church in prayer or a Bible reading at our first-ever ecumenical Thanksgiving worship service. Bussey's calm voice warned us that there was the possibility of trouble, though he reassured us: "But don't worry. It's only a rumor, and we will proceed as usual. We will not be intimated by this threat, and we will worship as we please."

That Thanksgiving morning, my mother, busily cooking, was glad to see my sisters and me get out of the house. We left home later than planned for church. As I parked the car and rushed toward the side door, I saw a ten-foot-tall wooden cross planted in the ground. And then, more shocking, there were men on horseback wearing tall, pointed dunce hats and white sheets. They were surrounding the cross to the left of the front entrance. My breathing quickened as we hurried safely into the building.

In church, I found the pew we regularly occupied on Sundays and breathed deeply. We were safe, but then minutes later, the men in white sheets walked straight down the aisle and sat down in pews close to the front of the altar, just opposite our side of the church. Mr. Bussey welcomed one and all to the church service and continued to proceed calmly. We rose and sang loudly "We Gather Together to Ask the Lord's Blessing" and then sat back down. When the Black minister moved to the pulpit up front and began to read from the Bible, the klansmen stood and paraded out. They could not stop the worship. I held my breath, intensely scared that the ministers, both of them, would be shot dead.

When we walked out of church, the thirty or so men on horseback had disappeared and taken their cross with them. I couldn't recall if we discussed the incident over lunch with my family. I was careful not to show my feelings. Though I could taste the fear in my throat, my mouth stayed closed. After all, like many in our community, Daddy had a gun case full of rifles and a pistol next to his bed.

THE FOLLOWING SCHOOL year, now living in a different upperclassman dorm, I didn't see Shirley or Carol Battle on campus, though I looked for them. When I went home on the weekends, I interjected my thoughts on other related issues. My parents knew I didn't believe that Martin Luther King was a Communist like they did. After one too many "looks," warnings from my mother, and my father's rage, I became invisible right before their very eyes.

In the fall of 1968, my last quarter in college, I met Kate Green, a freshman from Philadelphia, who offered me the perfect solution. It was God opening a window and me breathing for the first time since I was sixteen. Kate said I needed to move north where her parents would provide me with a haven, a roof over my head. Man, my bags were practically packed. I had no choice but to escape. Clearly, I was a danger to my family and to myself if I stayed. Kate and her family were Quakers. As pacifists, they did not own guns and were believers in the civil rights of all people.

At the end of January, I went home for a few days. On February 3, 1969, I arrived in New York City, where I lived for thirty-three years, returning to Wilson as a regular visitor, but free at last!

YEARS LATER, A friend at work, who had attended college in North Carolina, showed me a newspaper clipping. She was inspired by the retelling of a Thanksgiving Day service and a few brave ministers, including one Black pastor, in a small-town, mostly White community who would not allow the KKK to disrupt their first ecumenical worship service. With about 250 attendees, including a dozen or so Blacks, the article characterized this as "the first racially integrated program of speakers in a White church in this tobacco community of twenty thousand population." The article was complete with a picture of the cross and the horsemen parading in front of my church. Flabbergasted, I thought, I would never have known that our small town of Wilson could have ever made national news . . . but it did. I believe the clipping was cut from the *New York Times*, but I haven't been able to confirm it.

Postscript

On Sunday, June 26, 2022, I saw Pastor Bussey's youngest daughter, Marcia, and asked if she'd ever read the *New York Times* article about that historic day. She didn't know the article existed. Perhaps her father didn't know either, but he was deceased.

Marcia explained what happened around the dinner table following the service: "I was only seven years old that Thanksgiving. I thought those four men wearing the white pointed hats and robes were the Holy Spirit. When I asked my parents why they left the service early, my parents just broke down and had a good laugh!"

Today at the Wilson Public Library, I scanned the November and early December 1964 editions of the *Wilson Daily Times* and discovered a front-page article inviting the community to a Thanksgiving worship service, listing the names of all participating ministers. However, no coverage of the Thanksgiving Day incident ever appeared in our local newspaper. Apparently, the FBI had infiltrated the community and a small article appeared in the *New York Times* on November 28, 1964.

In an earlier *New York Times* article published on July 15, 1964, I read in detail about the fire at Shirley's Elm City Presbyterian Church. A few nights before the painting of the church began, the KKK's Grand Dragon organized 450 painters, with brushes and forty gallons of paint, and offered their services to avoid having the two races working side by side. The Grand Dragon threatened the safety of a group of painters, Whites, who had arrived from out-of-state.

That prompted North Carolina Governor Terry Sanford to act, and he brought in forty state troopers to ensure that no one was injured while the church was being painted by an integrated team of ministers and students. Other sources indicate two surveillance airplanes constantly circled overhead while the Black and White painters worked. Roads were policed and closed off. The small church had a membership of eight Blacks. The town of 729 had only two police officers, and the two men who tried to set the church on fire came from another town ten miles away.

WHILE SOME OF the details of my conversation with Shirley were fuzzy, I clearly remembered the terror she felt the night of the random threat of fire and the distinct feeling that she was being watched, which lasted long after the church was painted. So much of what happened during those early days of the Civil Rights Movement may be lost. Some of these stories never showed up in print until years later. Until the Klan took enough destructive action and the truth could no longer be swept firmly under the rug, the history of this nation was slowly reshaped.

Growing up in Wilson allowed for murmurs and small acts of discontentment. The history of my current divided town of fifty thousand is always evolving. I try to feel for a pulse. Will there be more eruptions, more rioting? The local newspaper struggles to survive, strives to unite the Black community with the Whites. Most neighborhoods are now integrated. A different war is going on: families are struggling to survive, divided by drugs, politics, and an intergenerational disconnection. I am watching it as it happens—and unlike many of my forebearers, I refuse to be silent.

ADULTHOOD

BE GOOD, BOYS, MOMMY WILL BE BACK SOON

by Stephanie Cowell

I SEARCH MY memories of which stories I would like to tell of my glorious, chaotic, not very lucrative singing career, a valiant effort to support my two sons sometimes singing opera (which didn't pay much) and ballads everywhere. I sang in several languages and accompanied myself on the guitar. My hair was loose, and I wore long dresses that swept to the floor. I made notes in the back of my hand diary of how much money was coming in that month and when I'd have enough for the rent.

Around 1980, I was a single mom with no child support living in a large Upper West Side (in Manhattan) building in a rent-stabilized apartment. My two sons, James and Jesse, were then about eight and eleven, and I often left them with a young babysitter at a friend's house, or sometimes for a few hours alone. I promised if I sang at enough places or earned enough money, I could buy them the sneakers they wanted. They were very enthusiastic about that, and my oldest, James, solemnly said, "I swearily promise to be good."

They were very thin, quick boys whom I loved with all my heart. This morning, like most others, I roused them from their slumbers and set out Cream of Wheat in two bowls on the worn sofa table near the worn leather sofa. We received everything thirdhand or found bargains in thrift shops. I sent the boys to school and then checked my little datebook for the location of my singing job for that day. It was Kings County Psychiatric Hospital, from a contract through the city to sing for the patients. I rolled my flowing dress in a shopping bag, took my guitar in its black case, and set off for Brooklyn.

"Be good boys," I reminded them at breakfast. And my youngest, Jesse, said warningly, "If anything starts, my brother started it." They had a series of ominous things they accused each other of. "Ma, he breathed on my comic book." "Ma, he's looking at me."

AFTER AN HOUR on the subway, I stood in the middle of a huge ward of wrought-iron hospital beds, having changed from my skirt and shirt into my dress. The director walked before me with a brisk tapping of her shoes. I was stunned by the high height of the ceiling and the bleakness. Though I had sung in different settings, I had never seen such a place. Sedated people drifted over the floor in long white nightgowns or pajamas.

Years later, in 2010, it was temporarily closed when authorities found abuse of patients, inadequate treatment, and dilapidated and filthy facilities. I could have told them that thirty years before when we approached a stick of an old woman curled in the bed, comatose.

The cheerful director gently shook the bony shoulder, and said, "Mary, this nice woman is here to sing for you."

I asked hesitantly in a soft voice, "How long has she been here?"

"Oh, near forty years. Isn't that so, Mary?"

I went through ward after ward that day, doors locked behind me. My voice was high and pure, and the lovely melody of the sixteenth-century English song "Greensleeves" floated through the rooms. I kept the horror and tears in my body, though afterward I often wondered, despairingly, why I had gone there. My little notes affirmed that I almost had the rent money. And I remembered the remarks of one tragic old man who likely had little left in his life to make him joyful. He looked at me tenderly and said, "Like an angel, you sing."

I came home on the rattling, grungy subway, which clattered and bumped through tunnels, and emerged somehow on the streets of Manhattan. A quarter in a corner phone booth brought the voice of my son James. "Hello, Mom!"

"Hello, darling. Is everything all right?"

"Yeah, we're watching television."

"There's pizza money in the kitchen. I'll be home later."

"Always singing," he muttered in his sweet, angular voice.

I said, "Don't get into any trouble."

"Okay," he said. "The babysitter's here."

AT THE LEGENDARY, high society 21 Club on West 52ⁿᵈ Street, I walked gravely up the steps past the many painted cast-iron jockey statues. Still in my tote bag was the very dress that trailed over the floors of the hospital a few hours before. I was hungry and just in time for a cocktail party for an executive of Philip Morris. In the pink-walled ladies' room, I changed from a skirt and blouse to the woman with the floating hair and high notes.

As they munched their canapés, I moved between them, singing my German and Italian folksongs, my Elizabethan melodies. How startling it was to be in a wood-paneled room! I still felt haunted by where I had been.

"Can you sing something from old England?" a woman asked, and I sang "Greensleeves." The woman who had hired me led me to the dining room for a free meal. I told her about my children and looked at the menu with some alarm. A spinach side dish was six dollars, enough to feed my little family for a day. I ate it as if putting my fork into gold. She paid for a plate of little cakes for me to take home to my sons.

I OPENED MY apartment door as always with trepidation, but all was well. My sons were quietly watching television, turning innocent faces to me. I asked them about school and homework. Pizza crusts sat curled on the sofa table. I paid the babysitter.

But when I went into their bedroom, I was surprised to find one of those huge beanbag chairs.

"We found it in the street and carried it up," James said proudly. "It just has a few small holes in it."

Good. Nothing had happened, just the acquisition of a pathetic old chair. It was probably filthy, but it was too late to take it away.

But (there was always going to be a "but" in this story, right?) I should have known. Still, I could never have conceived of the way boys' minds work and what they could do.

The next day, the boys swore they'd be good, and I let them come home two hours before me. When I arrived there with my arms full of groceries, the porter, Danny, came running across the lobby of my large building. Danny was a meticulous, small man who always felt with all the moral strength within him that what he cleaned should remain clean.

He cried, "Mrs., Mrs. I have just cleaned the courtyard below your window, and when I came out, I thought it was snowing."

"Snowing?" I asked, bewildered. It was a mild spring day. He closed the gate of the elevator up to my floor.

"From your window," he insisted.

My heart pounded as I inserted the key to my door.

The entire living room was strewn with small pieces of Styrofoam among a sea of beans. They floated, they drifted, they clustered around chair legs. Immediately, my sons crowded around me, saying, at once, "It's his fault . . . he made me do it," and punched each other.

While I had been away at a late rehearsal singing divine bits of Mozart with my concert group, the boys had decided that the best thing to do with the old beanbag chair was to enlarge the holes and throw the stuffing out the window. I leaned a little out the window, careful as we were seven floors up. Sure enough, the static beans clung to the brick side of the building all the way down to the courtyard.

"Danny just cleaned it," James said.

And indeed, the poor porter kept saying remorsefully, "Mrs., Mrs."

I found my wallet and gave him ten dollars. He retreated, mumbling about how women should stay home with their little monsters.

I returned to the living room.

"We'll help you clean it," Jesse said, sensing that perhaps they had made a wrong judgment about the holes and the chair and the so-called stuffing. I think he sensed I no longer wanted to hear how his brother had forced him.

We tried to clean it up. As I swept, the pieces flew away. I dropped handfuls into garbage bags. Chunks clung to my long hair and our clothes. We got out the vacuum, which ate tons of beans before expiring. It was a cheap vacuum cleaner.

I think it was years before we found the very last of the beans. My repentant sons had dragged the now-unstuffed chair downstairs, and of course they left a mess all along the basement corridor out to the garbage and the porter didn't speak nicely to me for weeks.

Later that evening, I rinsed my flowing light singing dress and hung it in the bathroom to dry. I had another job in three days and until then I was home cleaning or out shopping, being Mommy, and making quite sure my sons didn't get into trouble, which they generally did, anyway.

Somewhere in my mind, memories of those days cling to each other like the bits of foam beans: the hundreds of places I sang, the doors harshly locking behind me when I performed in prisons, the exquisite house parties with catered dinners, the penthouses, the basement senior centers, all the schools with children gathered around me, and the deformed old woman in a nursing home who asked if I sang in the key of E or F.

"We were monsters," James said recently when we talked about those times.

And Jesse, now in his forties, shook his head and muttered seriously, "But my brother really started everything."

The jury is still out on that.

Stephanie after performance, circa 1980.

Stephanie at twenty-five.

THE WORST POSSIBLE NEWS

by Linda Aronovsky Cox

WHEN I TALKED to Mom on the phone, she tried to soothe my fears. "I'm sure it will be okay," she murmured. But I knew she was wrong. I knew it would *not* be okay. And I was right.

It was November 9, 1994. I had just turned forty and had an almost nine-month-old infant, conceived after three years of infertility treatments. Fourteen months earlier, while I was pregnant, my then-husband, Mike, was diagnosed with early-stage esophageal cancer. He endured chemotherapy and radiation and was considered cancer-free just in time for Hallie's birth. But two months later, the cancer recurred with a vengeance, now Stage II, and he then had to undergo major surgery (the removal of most of his esophagus), which resulted in complications causing nerve damage and paralysis in his right arm.

I spent most of my maternity leave caring for a colicky baby who cried continuously unless I held her, and a sick and depressed husband who, with a paralyzed arm, needed help with daily activities.

When I returned to work, my focus remained on my demanding baby and my distraught husband undergoing cancer treatment. I was determined to be the dutiful wife and mother, as well as the consummate professional. The superwoman who could do it all.

The stress was enormous. Little did I know then the stiff price I would pay.

The Grim Diagnosis

For some time, as I nursed Hallie, I noticed my left breast looked different, the nipple and skin changing, but I was sure it was related to nursing. Plus, I was too busy to worry about it. Finally, after complaining to a friend, she insisted I call my doctor immediately. I made an appointment with my ob/gyn for that Monday.

He examined me and thought it wise to see a specialist. Two days later, the breast surgeon did a needle biopsy. It was excruciating. When it was over, I sat up, and he looked at me and said these exact words: "I don't want to sound dramatic, but this presents itself as breast cancer."

I knew that no doctor would say this unless the symptoms were so clear he or she was certain of the diagnosis; and in my case, they were. He said my type of breast cancer was so aggressive that it had probably started only six months earlier, right after my postpartum checkup and while my husband was fighting for his life in the ICU. He later said it was likely triggered by the massive stress I had been under, like an atomic bomb exploding in my breast, not like the slow-growing masses of most breast cancers.

The next day, Thursday, November 10, 1994, he called with the official biopsy results. Mike took the call, as I hovered in the bathroom, afraid to listen in, but I could hear him repeating "aggressive," "serious," "start chemo immediately."

I did not have the typical breast cancer. No, I had to get the worst kind there was. Inflammatory Breast Cancer (IBC) manifests in the skin causing redness, swelling, and skin puckering (called *peau d'orange*), usually without a mass. It is the rarest (only about 4 percent of all cases), most aggressive, and most deadly form of breast cancer with the worst prognosis—two out of three who get it die within five years.

Because of its virulence, I had to start chemotherapy the next morning, only four days after I first went to the doctor. That night, I nursed Hallie for the last time. I had planned on nursing for years. I cried. I would miss this the most.

Ironically, this was exactly one week before Mike's final chemo session. I was already planning our trip to celebrate and hoping to have another child. Both wishes were now crushed.

Earlier that day, we had seen Mike's oncologist at the clinic, where I had accompanied him for the past year. The doctor had already spoken to the breast surgeon. As bad as it was, he was optimistic and hopeful. Not even one day had passed and these two doctors were planning to do everything they could to save my life.

A Poor Prognosis

One month later, I sat in a small examination room at the University of Texas Health Science Center in San Antonio facing one of the top breast-cancer researchers in the country, who I was consulting for an evaluation and second opinion. Following a physical exam and a day-long study of my files, he came to his conclusion.

He looked directly at me and pronounced, "You have a very poor prognosis." I was stunned. I knew it was bad, but I was in shock at hearing those words. I don't remember much after that. I know he discussed the aggressiveness of IBC, the large mass (estimated at 8-12 cm), the advanced staging (III-B, the highest before metastasis). I had no more than a 35 percent chance of surviving five years, he said.

I thanked him. My friend, there for moral support, was also shocked. I was numb. I knew I would soon crumble into a thousand pieces. I just wanted to go home to my husband and hold my beloved daughter.

From that day on, I cried every night. I would hold Hallie in the rocking chair for hours while she slept, weeping uncontrollably.

The Grueling Treatment

Seated in a circle with a group of women at the American Cancer Society's second-ever support group in Austin for women with breast cancer, I was with a friend who had just been diagnosed. Neither of us knew anyone our age who had breast cancer.

The women were fretting about the decisions they had to make— lumpectomy or mastectomy? One side or bilateral? Chemotherapy or radiation?

I chuckled to myself, because none of this was relevant. My cancer was so serious that I had to undergo the maximum of all possible treatments. I was fighting for my life, so these discussions seemed rather trivial to me, though I realized they were profound for these much-older women. They all sympathized deeply with the seriousness of what I was facing.

The plan was simple. Four rounds of chemotherapy, three weeks apart, from November 1994 to January 1995, followed by a mastectomy in February. Then a new procedure for breast cancer, high dose chemotherapy with a stem cell transplant at a hospital in San Antonio in March or April, after I recovered from surgery. Once I regained strength, I'd undergo thirty-eight rounds of daily radiation in August and September. Finally, in December, when I recovered from radiation, I would have reconstructive surgery. I had just started my journey of more than a year of unremitting, arduous treatment.

With Hallie's first birthday coming up in February, I timed the mastectomy surgery for the week after her party. The breast surgery went well, but two weeks later I suddenly developed bacteremia, a severe bacterial blood infection that put me back in the hospital and on antibiotic IV infusions for weeks. I had to postpone the stem cell transplant. I could have died from sepsis.

Lethal Chemotherapy

The worst aspect of the stem cell procedure was not the weeks-long hospitalization in isolation, or the severe side effects from the massive chemo dosages.

No, the very worst was when I arrived at the hospital transplant center in San Antonio, and they had to put the infusion port *in my neck*! "No, not my neck," I begged. I was horrified and felt overwhelmingly vulnerable.

I cried as they inserted the four-pronged port into the right side of my neck, to allow the simultaneous infusion of four deadly drugs directly into my heart.

The stem cell procedure—technically called "high-dose chemotherapy with autologous stem cell transplantation"—allows delivery of a lethal dosage of chemotherapy to address potential micrometastases (undetected cancer on the cellular level). It is lethal in that all blood cells are also destroyed—red cells (oxygen), white (immunity), and platelets (blood clotting), leaving the patient with zero immunity or strength. Then, one's own stem cells that have been previously harvested are infused to redevelop into the three blood cell types, minus any dormant cancer cells remaining in the body. That was the hope.

I lay in bed for four days with the drugs pouring into me. I was lucky—my stem cells grew back quickly and strongly, in the top 10 percent of patients my doctor said. I only had to spend another two weeks in the hospital, then return home to gain strength. I was completely depleted, unable to do the simplest physical activity. It took three months to recover, and then the eight weeks of daily radiation treatments began.

Protected by Leonard

I first saw him as I lay on the hard table that had been cranked up high by the technicians, bringing me closer to the huge radiation apparatus that towered over me. I held my arm outstretched over my head as they directed long thick metal arms to targeted positions tattooed on my chest, chatting and joking for the thirty-minute duration. I didn't feel human, just a job to be done.

I was tired, bone tired. My arm ached. I hated this. Even after everything I had been through for the past ten months, this was the worst. Doesn't make sense, but does any of this?

And then sometime early on, I saw him. A great eagle perched high above on the machine, looking down at me. He knew I was afraid, and he was there to protect me. And I knew his name was Leonard.

Leonard the eagle appeared to me every day from then on. His presence was reassuring, letting me know I was safe and going to be okay. He reminded me I could do this and helped quell my fears.

Leonard made the remainder of my time there bearable. I still hated it. I was still tired, my arm still ached, but he was always there, shielding and safeguarding me. Under his watch, I felt strengthened.

A New Breast

Mike didn't care. In fact, he couldn't believe I wanted to go through with it. But I noticed that Hallie, now nearly two, would stare at my chest, focused on the asymmetry. And I knew that if I had something that looked like a real breast, maybe I could somehow forget what I was dealing with. Without reconstruction, I could never escape the reminder. It was more than a year after my diagnosis, the last step in my breast cancer journey. I wanted this badly.

Because implants had been taken off the market for leakage, the only option at the time was the tram-flap procedure—major surgery, lengthy and difficult, with a protracted recovery period. It uses abdominal skin and tissue, leaving it attached to the abdominal muscle to maintain a blood supply, which is then tunneled upward under the skin to the reopened surgical scar and formed into a breast.

I woke after the surgery and felt the full impact of the incisions on my chest and across my entire lower abdomen, hip to hip (a tummy-tuck!), and the rearranged abdominal muscle. I could not turn or bend or sit up without help. I could barely move at all.

As much as I had wanted it, I then realized how disabling this surgery was. What was I thinking? And with an active toddler at home, who I couldn't lift for months.

Recovery was long and difficult but recover I did. Despite the initial distress, I was delighted with the results.

I Made It

Five years later, I had beaten the odds. I was still alive. I was told that if I could reach the magic five-year marker, I was likely home free because with IBC's aggressiveness, it would have recurred quickly. Hallie had started school, and I greedily wanted to see her through all her life stages and even play with grandchildren.

This was the mid-1990s. Virtually no breast cancer support or resources. No internet. Little information was available. The only reliable and informative breast cancer book at the time was *Dr. Susan Love's Breast Book*, where there were only three pages on IBC, basically saying it was a death sentence. That is all I had to go on.

But I was determined to live. And I survived these twenty-eight years not because of my attitude, motivation, strength, or lifestyle, not due to others' prayers or any other factor (though these certainly helped me cope). Cancer is bigger than all of that. It kills a lot of people who do everything right.

I was just lucky. Miraculously, I lived.

With baby Hallie before Linda lost her hair to chemo (prior to mastectomy), November 1994.

Grown-up Hallie with Linda, November 2014.

PLANS A, B, AND C

by Jane Mylum Gardner

PLAN A

Ten months after the bombing of the World Trade Center, I could read the writing on the wall. Jobs like mine in the financial world were evaporating. Business as usual no longer existed. There was a new norm.

My boss Russ warned me, "Rumor has it that layoffs are coming soon." Although he had seniority, he was biting his fingernails. "You need to be making plans," Russ whispered on a 99-degree day in mid-July.

I wanted out of New York, frightened by the constant presence of cops on street corners and the prevailing terror atmosphere. I couldn't take much more of waiting for another attack or the axe to fall. All I wanted was my old life back, my life as it was on September 10, 2001. I was barely making it.

I panicked. There was no Plan B, only Plan A, which was to stay in my rut. But, on a lark that same afternoon, I cruised the internet to check out art teaching jobs in North Carolina, my home state. I figured there would be nothing available this close to the start of the school year. August 5th, the first day of school, was only three weeks away. But *voila*! There was one art teaching position open in my hometown of Wilson, and all I had to do was hit "send" after I attached my resume. I thought nothing of it. The job was most likely filled and not yet removed from the vacancy list. My salary would be cut deeply, but I would not starve as my parents still lived in town. I needed protection.

Even though I wasn't sure if my teaching license was still valid, I hit "send." I forgot about it until two days later. Then, after a long day at work, I arrived home to find a message from Mr. Brad Shackelford, principal at Speight Middle School, asking me to call him. After two interviews, fingerprinting, and a background check, including two separate trips to North Carolina, Mr. Shackelford offered me the job.

"Be there, when?" I asked.

"Next week."

PLAN B

I had no time to think about it. I had always known I'd go back home, having been groomed as the oldest child to take care of my parents. And perhaps it was better this way. Some friends were shocked, others were not. I called my landlord. My sisters arrived to pack up my entire household into a U-Haul and to help move my life 650 miles to a storage unit. I arrived a few days after school started.

Though I felt ill-equipped to teach art to 340 middle-school children, I knew how to land on my feet. However, I soon learned that no matter how much I tried, this job was a close-to-impossible task. It was not calm and quiet like my old proofreading job. It was loud and noisy. I slowly learned to understand the children's strong southern accents and could decipher what they were saying. I hadn't written a lesson plan since college graduation thirty-three years earlier, but I could follow instructions.

Sunday was family day. After my sisters had had a proper Sunday lunch at Parker's Barbecue, they would show up with their husbands and children at my parents' house as I rushed out the door to get home, grade papers, and write lesson plans. Rarely did they call and invite my parents and me to join them; I was relieved, as fried hush puppies were not healthy to begin with. Still, I felt left out.

Sunday night was the worst because it took most of the weekend to figure out what the hell I was going to teach in the upcoming week. I'd think of Monday morning when I'd be standing in front of thirty-five disrespectful eighth graders who were only there because there was no study hall offered and the administration had to place these kids somewhere. Art, like music, was of no academic value in the eyes of many.

The stress in my body grew as I struggled to teach from an art textbook and to match interesting lesson ideas to a season, holiday, and the art skills outlined in *The North Carolina Standard Course of Study*. I soon realized that all that was needed was a warm body standing in the front of the class to make sure the kids were not fighting or feeling each other up in the back row of the classroom.

Discipline problems were not acceptable to Mr. Brad Shackelford. "Call their parents!" he said.

They replied, "You handle it! I can't do nothin' with him at home either!"

I ate lunch many days with the music teacher, whose classroom was also used as a dumping ground. Academic teachers needed to eat lunch, have a bathroom break, and a class period to call parents and to plan.

I tried my best. I showed up every day, I called parents, I hung artwork all over the school, I held exhibits, and entered kids' work in contests. I spent summers recovering and planning. I'd tell myself, "You can do this."

All the while, my sisters got angrier and angrier at me, because I wanted them to participate more in family life, not just drop by for a Sunday afternoon visit. They thought I had come home because I was finally taking on the responsibility of being a daughter, who had no other distractions like a husband to care for. They seemed emotionally removed from Daddy, who had been on suicide watch at the hospital, numb to his depression and his cancer treatments.

Before I ever hit "send" on that computer in July 2002, I should have made a phone call to say, "I will consider coming home if you think we're going to be a family again." But I had been in a panic mode. My sisters had husbands and homes. They had good jobs and children. I didn't have their sense of security, and they had not lived through the terror of September 11th. Though I'd had a fairly wonderful life living in New York for thirty-three years, I was plagued with guilt for not being home.

My sisters never said it was now my turn to "just handle it." Their actions spoke louder. They cared little about the friends I left behind or what life had been like for me. They simply dropped the ball in my lap and slammed the door in my face.

I helped both of my parents gracefully survive the last years of their lives. Daddy lived for almost a year after I left New York and Mama died in August 2017, fifteen years later.

During the fourteen years I taught art, some fourteen hundred middle-school children and five thousand students in elementary school walked through my classroom door. Some of my former students never stopped appreciating what I passed on to them and have become art teachers and professionals in the arts. Others may very well be sitting in jail or are dead from drug overdoses. I am always running into one of my students or reading about them in the newspaper.

PLAN C

Mother has been gone for five years now, and my life is slowly taking a new direction. I have fallen in love with my garden and the church where I play handbells. During the pandemic, neither one of my sisters called, even when they knew I had pneumonia. I no longer served a purpose in their lives, and we rarely spoke. The cold, one-way street relationship I felt with them was a dead end.

Zoom reunited me with my friends in New York, who introduced me to abstract art. After not painting for forty-five years, I am an artist now. I am finally painting about the bombing of the World Trade Center.

Plan C is emerging, and I am giving more thought to what I want to do with the rest of my life. Plans A and B were history. Moving forward with the support of friends means leaving behind a family that was injured by alcoholism and narcissism, a difference in political values and life experiences.

Yes, I am different from my North Carolina family despite repeatedly trying to fit in. I remain an outcast; phone calls are sometimes not returned. No time, no apologies. It is still hard to walk away, but I can choose courage. At seventy-five, I have a grateful heart, but a deep sadness.

"We are shaped both by our mothers' yearnings and our desperate need to break free of them. The dynamic between these two powerful forces is largely what molds our lives as women." — Erica Jong

TWO TYPES OF PEOPLE

by Karen Finch

"THERE ARE TWO types of people in the world: givers and takers. I've always thought of you as a giver."

My mother said that to me as we sat in a waiting room ahead of a family conference with both my children's therapists; Mum being the other parental figure who was mostly in their lives following my divorces. My brother's partner was due to have a baby, and they were gathering things to prepare for the birth. He'd asked Mum for the bassinet. *My* bassinet, bought by my godmother when I was born. Of course, my brother slept in it as a tiny baby too, but when I had my first child, Mum gave it to me.

She said that to me after I'd been hesitant about handing it over. Justifiably, I felt. Since childhood, my brother has stolen from me, broken treasured possessions, or not returned borrowed items. Nothing ever came back to what it had been.

I got my first job when I was fifteen, working after school and on Saturday mornings at a local florist. Looking back, it paid little, but that money was mine. I was saving it and had a stash hidden in the back corner of my wardrobe. I hadn't decided what I was saving for, but I felt so rich as it added up slowly. I remember getting home from work one Saturday and going to the wardrobe to add that week's pay to the stash. Only it was gone. All of it. Some seventy odd dollars. Weeks and weeks of work. I told Mum. She said I should have put it in the bank. The money never reappeared.

I had reminded her of that, and other incidents. I also suggested that, knowing I had the bassinet, it would have been more appropriate for my brother to ask me himself, and questioned why she'd been the one.

"He thought you might not want him to have it," she said. That was when I got the "two types of people in the world" speech.

In hindsight, Mum did that a lot—divide the world into two types of people. It always irritated me because it was so very black and white. The world, to me, is a very gray place.

She used it to make sense of things that she struggled with emotionally, especially if there were other parties involved. In this bassinet instance, she wanted me to be the "good" girl, the kind and generous one who could forgive her brother a lifetime of indifference, abuse, lies, theft, and provocation that ultimately left *me* in trouble. Not that she'd ever articulated that. Because my mother was the chatelaine of the world's biggest cupboard full of skeletons. She stuffed all the nasties of my lifetime in there, along with hers, my brother's, my father's, and other family members.

What she didn't want was a daughter who forced her, as I did that afternoon, to confront reality. She didn't want me to bring up all those past resentments—*again*. Resentments that could have been ameliorated by him apologizing and making amends.

"It's harder for your brother, dear. It's much harder for men and boys to apologize."

Oh. Right. That's why he could do awful stuff and not suffer any consequences, but I couldn't. That's why my mother expected me to do the right thing, and then some, as if none of those things had happened.

"You mustn't be so angry, dear! Just calm down."

And then my father would do or say things that she had every right to be angry about, but she'd be calm. All that emotion, locked in the cupboard with the other skeletons.

"I am not like you," I said, as I told her so many times. I couldn't lock all that stuff away as she did. As a teenager, I told her. I told her as a new wife, struggling with the inequities of my marriage, and again when I had to leave, and yet again when I had to leave my second marriage. I told her as a mother, as I parented my boys with transparency, allowing them to see my sadness, frustrations, and anger along with the joy, wonder, and playfulness.

Mum's "two types of people" were always completely oppositional. So, if I was meant to be a giver, then being a taker was bad. But somehow, my brother, the taker, wasn't bad.

"Family is different, dear. You have to forgive him for those things."

Family is different? So, there were two sets of rules. One for family, and one for the rest of the world. People in the rest of the world who were arseholes could be rejected. But my brother, the taker, who was an arsehole . . . him, I had to make excuses for as Mum did, and keep in my life, allowing him to continue to disrupt it and cause me grief.

I ALSO REMINDED her of the time he dropped by my house without calling first, a strict rule I had for everyone as I was so busy working and studying while parenting alone. He found the kids there with their regular sitter and pushed his way into my house. He said he'd just play with the kids for a bit, then parked himself against a wall and chatted the sitter up. He wouldn't leave until she said she had to call me, as she was instructed not to allow anyone in the house when she was looking after the boys. So, he left. When I got home, she was still quite distressed. I called him and reminded him not to come over if I wasn't home, and that he made my sitter feel unsafe.

The next thing that happened was a phone call from Mum saying that my brother told her he wasn't allowed to go to my house anymore, and what the hell was that about? After she related his carefully edited account, I acquainted her with the full story and asked her why she felt it necessary to attack me first without asking me what had happened. There was a long silence in response to my question, followed by a muttered, "Oh well, he didn't tell me all of that." But no apology for the attack on me.

This was a situation so reminiscent of our childhood, when he'd dance in and out of my room, taunting and teasing, until I lost it and yelled at him. Then I'd be in trouble for yelling, while he disappeared before Mum appeared.

LATER IN THE session with the kids' therapists—a psychiatrist and a social worker—the violence that had been part of my eldest's acting out came up. The psychiatrist noted my discomfort and addressed it, asking why I was so distressed. I said it was bringing back too many memories of the fear I felt growing up with a violent father and sibling.

Mum jumped in. "I wouldn't say they were violent. They were both angry sometimes, but I wouldn't call them violent."

I couldn't let her jam that skeleton back into the cupboard. I wanted it *in* the room. I was bringing up two boys who would one day be men, who had their own grief and anger over the losses they'd experienced. And

I wanted them dealt with so that history wouldn't cycle back around on them. And here she was, trying to shut me down again.

So, I pushed. And it was hard. But it was honest. Honesty, emotional honesty, is hard, especially with no one to learn it from. Mum's type of honesty was just the day-to-day stuff about not lying. It had little to do with honesty about feelings. It was all about taking the path of least resistance, and not rocking the boat—any boat. I'm not built like that. I have no poker face, so people know what I'm feeling even if I don't say. And when I do, it's impulsive, because I can't *not* say . . . where Mum always thought carefully before she spoke, maintaining a neutral expression, even when someone might have really upset her.

I DID HAND the bassinet over to my brother, but not until Mum promised she'd get it and bring it back to me as soon as her imminent grandchild had a cot to sleep in. I didn't include all the linen I'd made for it. My brother took his time returning it via my mother.

There are two types of people in the world. There are those of us who ask questions even when we're scared. Because it's safer to acquire the knowledge that enables us to make better choices. And then there are the ones like my mum who put all those sad, traumatic, emotional things in a cupboard with the skeletons, and hope that they can't get out.

WRITING INTO THE FEAR

by Kathleen M. Rodgers

ALONE IN A crappy motel a half-mile from the Air Force base, I shook in fear as the television announcer proclaimed with a glaring headline across the screen, "United States Air Force Thunderbolt II A-10 crashes in the desert. Pilot killed."

Twenty-one years old and newly married to a fighter pilot stationed at the base, I waited for a knock at the door or a note from the motel office (our room had no telephone that October day in 1979), informing me that my groom of three weeks had crashed his single-seat fighter jet in the desert outside Tucson. Trembling and lightheaded, I felt helpless and alone. I saw visions of the crash site, nothing left of my fighter pilot, Tom, but a smoking hole among the towering saguaros standing sentinel for decades. We'd arrived at this place in the desert days after our wedding at a base chapel in New Mexico, my husband so dashing in his officer's dress uniform with combat medals and wings pinned over his heart.

This was my initiation into the "glamorous" world of the fighter pilot.

About an hour later, I heard the distinct rumble of my husband's Corvette as he rounded the corner of our motel and pulled into the parking slot in front of our room. I leaped from the bed and bolted out the door as he climbed out of the car, clad in his green flight suit and blue cap.

Hugging him tightly, I bawled like a baby into his warm neck, his scent reassuring as I blurted through tears, "I thought you were dead. An A-10 crashed in the desert. I thought it was you."

That day was a moment of reckoning for me as a young military wife. I learned that my "military dependent ID card" that ushered me into places of privilege where only service members and their families could go—i.e., the base exchange and commissary—could not protect me from the fact that it all could be taken away in an instant.

When a fighter jet crashes, there are usually no survivors unless the pilot ejects safely. Less than four months later, I would learn this lesson again when the pilot who played the trumpet at our wedding, one of my husband's best friends, was killed instantly back in New Mexico in an air mishap with his F-111. Six months later, it happened when another good friend of ours was killed in an air accident.

Pilots die in peacetime training missions, even when there are no wars going on. In one year alone, my husband lost eleven friends. This was before we got married. Looking back, I must've known this on some level, but it didn't sink in until I married into the military and knew pilots who died. Every day back then, when my hubby zipped up his flight suit and headed out the door for a flight, I didn't know if I would ever see him again.

I began to live in fear. The kind of fear that keeps you on guard any time your loved one is not with you. Back then, every time I left the house to run an errand or attend class, I dreaded turning up in my street. The first thing I checked was the curb and our driveway to make sure there was not a blue staff car with uniformed officers waiting to deliver the devastating news that my handsome pilot, the man of my dreams, was dead in a crash. His body burned beyond recognition or "twenty-five pounds of hamburger meat," a phrase used often in those days among pilots when talking about accidents.

The fear only increased over the years when I became a young mother of two sons. While the boys and I cheered our pilot on and waved our American flags and craned our necks skyward to watch a formation of fighter jets scream overhead, knowing Daddy might be one of them, I stuffed my terror deep inside to protect my sons. But my sons were smart, and they knew the risks, especially when Tom deployed to Saudi Arabia in 1990 after Iraq invaded Kuwait.

By then, I was building my portfolio as a freelance writer. Instead of avoiding the subject of what it meant to live in constant fear of sudden loss, I harnessed this energy into emotionally charged essays and cover stories for publications like *Military Times* and later *Family Circle*, a national magazine where millions read my work.

My goal all along was to elevate military service members and their families into the mainstream. I figured out how to introduce a military character or family member into an article or novel targeted at the civilian population.

Once my husband retired from the military and started flying for the airlines in 1991, I relaxed a bit. I didn't worry as much whenever he left the house to fly passengers from point A to point B. My anxieties transferred to raising sons and all the responsibilities that come with being a parent.

JUST WHEN I thought I'd finally left behind our military days, our youngest son graduated from college and became an army officer. Shortly after his commission, he deployed to Afghanistan. All the fear from my husband's military days came crashing back.

Two days after our son deployed, an editor from a top military online publication contacted me and asked me to write an essay about which was worse, sending a husband to war or a son? It took me less than five minutes to accept the assignment. I was tired of feeling paralyzed with my heart constantly jammed in my throat.

So, I did what I have learned to do over the decades: I wrote straight into the fear.

Here's an excerpt from part of the essay that was originally published on June 29, 2014, under the popular column, "SpouseBuzz" on Military. com. Used with permission:

> On a recent weekend, in a parking lot at Fort Hood, Texas, I stood with my family as we gathered to say farewell to my youngest son, J.P., a first lieutenant in the United States Army, as he prepared to deploy to an undisclosed location in the Middle East.
>
> Even though we were all smiling with pride, our hearts were already breaking. I held it together for the send-off, but I fell apart after we got back to the hotel.
>
> For me, sending a son to war is worse than sending a husband into harm's way. No matter how much you love your husband, you didn't wipe away his childhood tears or chase away the boogeyman hiding under the bed. You didn't cheer him on through freezing rain, eye-stinging dust storms, or blazing heat in sporting events that never seemed to end.
>
> Whether your child is five or twenty-five, mother love never changes. You might not take a bullet for your beloved, but you sure as hell would for your son.
>
> So once again, I am living with the unholy terror of a military staff car pulling up to my home. This time it's in a quiet civilian

neighborhood where we raised our sons since my husband left the military.

In May 2012, my son's roommate from Officer Candidate School was killed in action by an IED. From the moment our son called us with the news, the wars in Iraq and Afghanistan came crashing into our home. War is no longer some abstract action taking place halfway around the world where other people's grown children battle it out. War is personal, and my baby son is now in the thick of it.

In a parking lot at Fort Hood, surrounded by hundreds of soldiers and their families saying farewells, I watched my son interact with the men in his platoon. The little boy I once cradled and sang hymns to at night had turned into a grown man right before my eyes. He is a leader of men I would want to follow if I were going to war.

Yet even as I embraced him for one more hug, I already missed him.

Postscript

My son did return from war and went on another deployment to a different location. As a military spouse turned military mother, I can't help but think what other families in other nations are going through when war breaks out. My prayers as I write this are for the people of Ukraine.

Kathleen hugs son J.P. on his way to Afghanistan, 2014.

WHEN TEXAS LOST POWER

by Linda Aronovsky Cox

I AM STILL awake at 1:00 a.m. when the power goes out. It is Monday morning, February 16, 2021, and I get a news update on my phone that Austin Energy has announced rolling blackouts to allow the Texas electric grid to cope with the low temperatures across the state accompanying the winter storm. I huddle in bed under the covers, hoping the power will be restored soon.

In the morning, I wake up in a cold bedroom. The sun is shining, and the world has turned white overnight. I open my front door to look out. My car is completely encased in ice and snow. Miss Grace, my thirteen-year-old calico cat, runs to the porch as she does on her daily sojourns. She stops suddenly at the edge, startled at the sea of white before her. After a few moments, she darts off the porch, keeping to the perimeter of the house where there isn't much snow. She doesn't immediately return when I call her, so I leave her out, reminding myself to check on her in a few minutes.

It is cold. The back porch thermometer reads 12 degrees. Texas is not used to this. The inside thermostat says 58 degrees. That doesn't sound too bad, but it feels chilly since I normally set it at 68 or 70. I take a quick shower and wash my hair, a good choice because this is the last one I will have for four days.

I dress in my warmest sweater, the one I never wear in Texas, over a long-sleeved T-shirt for insulation and add a heavy cardigan, thick socks, my warmest slippers, and a shawl around my shoulders. I go to the kitchen and stop suddenly—I can't make coffee. There is only electricity in the kitchen here, no gas. Okay.

I check on Miss Grace. She is nowhere to be seen, but then I hear her meowing from the driveway of the house next door and see the little kitty paw prints she left in the snow. She paces back and forth on the edge of the driveway, mewling, begging for help. I run and get boots from my last visit north, put on my warmest coat, and venture gingerly onto the ice-covered snow, carefully traversing the lawn to rescue her. I scoop her up and bring her back to the relative warmth inside. Miss Grace hates the cold.

I settle down in my upholstered armchair. It's too cold to sit anywhere else. I wrap a quilt around my shoulders and snuggle under a blanket. I am warm and comfortable. I read.

I grab food out of the fridge for lunch. I don't think of putting the freezer contents outside or the refrigerator items in my garage, as others later tell me they did. I will have to toss everything when this is all over.

I check the power on my phone. Mostly charged. I find my three small power banks, and each has partial charges. That will have to do for now. My phone is my only connection with the world. I check the news, weather reports, energy updates. I send texts, checking on friends. Most are also without power, but many have gas stoves, so at least they can heat food or use the oven for heat.

By late Monday, I know there is nothing "rolling" about this blackout. The temperature drops when the sun goes down, and it is eerily dark, but I have plenty of flashlights. Inexplicably, I never think to light any of the many candles I own. I have an unused fireplace; I don't dare chance it now. It needs a chimney-sweep cleaning before next winter, I decide.

I head to bed at 8:30 p.m., extraordinarily early for this night owl. I get two wool blankets and place them over the woven blanket and quilt already there, and then top that with a heavy throw. I put on my warmest flannel nightgown, the one reserved for northern visits, my flannel robe, another pair of socks and gloves, and climb into the bone-chillingly cold bed. I curl into a fetal position until the bedding warms.

Miss Grace and Zuko, her sister, cuddle close, pressed into my chest and tummy. I'm their only source of warmth. Miss Grace curls into a tight ball and does not move the entire night.

Some days after the freeze ends, I see hanging in my closet the plush robe that I never wear because it makes me too hot. I was too befuddled to remember it when I was freezing.

DAY TWO, SAME as the day before. My car is still encased in snow and ice, and the ground is so icy it would be dangerous to venture onto the driveway. I dress warmly and huddle down in my armchair with the blankets around me. For lunch, I eat cold packages of pre-cooked rice and beans out of the pantry. I don't lack for food, just ways to heat it. I remind myself to get a small cookstove before next winter.

I monitor the news from Austin Energy and hear that they will start rolling power. At 5:00 p.m., I am startled when the lights suddenly return. I rush to plug in my phone and power banks and heat up leftover soup.

Then suddenly at 6:00 p.m., it is over. ERCOT, the power grid company that controls the system in Texas, ordered Austin Energy to shut it down. They're trying to prevent statewide collapse of the entire system. What?

TUESDAY NIGHT BEDTIME is the same as Monday's, but it is now colder in the house. My kitties and I hunker down together again. The unrelenting low temperatures outside continue to drop the inside temps, despite the relative tightness of my house—greatly appreciated during the blazing hot summers, never tested in the winter. I wake up the next morning to the thermostat reading 49 degrees. Ouch!

But it is another beautiful sunshiny day. The outside temperatures are close to zero, so the ice-covered snow remains thick, but the whiteness shines gloriously.

It is cold, achingly cold. There is not much to do except spend another day reading. Oh, throw me in that briar patch! I catch up on the *New York Times* book reviews and magazines and turn to my current book, *The Goldfinch* by Donna Tartt. I stay covered and blanketed in the armchair, further insulated by the upholstery surrounding me. I can't sit anywhere else and get warm.

I hear from friends who still have power offering their homes as a refuge. But my car is still covered with ice and the streets look impassable. And with the pandemic raging, I don't want to share non-socially distanced indoor car space with anyone, masked or otherwise. This is pre-vaccine time.

The online maps include the length of time without power, and I notice that mine no longer reads 1:00 a.m. Monday, when it started. It reads that it began Tuesday at 6:00 p.m., after the single measly hour of electricity. I am furious! They will restore power in order of who has been out the longest. Save one hour, that is me. I will complain loudly about the unfairness of this when it is over.

I am on Facebook a lot. It doesn't use a lot of cell phone power, and many of my friends are posting, so we can all complain and compare notes.

IT IS NOW Wednesday, more than fifty-five hours without power. With the sun shining, the ice does not look as foreboding, and I venture out to unseal my car. I carefully step across the treacherous, ice-covered driveway. I use a broom handle to break off the icicles and ice and then the straw end to sweep off the snow. I discover an ice scraper in the garage and begin that task. And then *voila*! When I pull the door handle, it pops open.

I start the car. I plug in my phone and a power bank, listen to NPR, and crank on the heat. It is rather cozy. When I look at the gas gauge, I note that I should have filled it up before it fell below the one-quarter mark. Too late now, but this will keep me from running the car too long.

I make a mental note to clear out half the garage so I can park in there. That would have made it easier to use the car for warmth and get frequent power recharges throughout the day. But who would have thought that would be a good reason?

Friends text me, offering to come rescue me with their trucks, but I decline. I can't leave my cats. Plus, pandemic.

WEDNESDAY NIGHT BEDTIME is a repeat of the previous two nights. The cold is pervasive and has settled into my bones. But I think about the homeless living in tents all over Austin with the repeal of the bans. I think about low-income elderly who have poorly insulated homes. I think about those who depend on electricity for life-sustaining medical care. I think about mothers with babies and young children. What are they doing? How are they adjusting?

I realize that I am not suffering. I am merely uncomfortable, inconvenienced, bored. I can live with this. I accept my reality. I am not happy, but I have no real worries. I feel resilient. I am focused on what is happening right now, and it's enough to sustain me.

Thursday, the thermostat still reads 49 degrees. The insulation is holding, thankfully, keeping the temperature from dropping even lower. Cold, very, very cold, but it could be worse. I later learn that my next-door neighbor's inside temperature dropped to 32 degrees.

I don't eat much; I have little appetite. I don't think much; my brain feels like it's in a fog. All I do is sit and focus on staying warm, cuddling the cats, reading. It is forced mindfulness.

The day before, Austin Water lost a treatment plant when the equipment froze, so now many residents are without water. They advise people to use melted snow to flush their toilets. For those with water, there is a boil-water notice. I am lucky—I never lost water, which is good because I have no way to boil it. And even if I did, I maintain a stockpile so I wouldn't have run out.

As the fourth day passes, some of my friends report that their power has been restored. Not me. I was out longer than they were, but because of the freak single hour, the maps no longer show that. At 8:00 p.m., I prepare to post on Facebook that I am getting ready to go to bed for my *fifth* freezing-cold night without power. And then suddenly, like magic, poof! The lights come on. My neighborhood is among the last in the city to be restored.

THE NEXT DAY, I look around to assess the damage. Outside in my front garden beds, the gigantic prickly pear cacti are shriveled and flattened to the ground. Several large branches of my spectacular mountain laurel tree bend to the ground from the weight of the ice and look partially dead. The huge rosemary plants are decimated. All the well-established aloe vera plants along the front are gone. It is hard to tell with the rest. Landscapers and gardeners are advising not to pull anything up yet, to wait and see what might come back. Fortunately, I had brought the potted plants into the garage, and they all survived.

Amazingly, the prolonged freeze somehow stimulated the growth of my red oak, which quickly grew taller with the branches spreading far. And much to my surprise, a sea of sunflowers and lantana appeared in the front garden bed where the now-deserted cacti and other plants had previously thrived.

The following summer, as the temperatures approached 100 degrees, state power grid officials and Austin Energy asked residents to keep our air-conditioning thermostats high to minimize power use, afraid the grid would fail again. And now we face another winter. Nothing has changed. I best start getting ready.

IN ADDITION TO remembering a cookstove, my plush robe, candles, clean garage, full tank of gas, fridge and freezer outdoor storage, and ready fireplace, this is what I know: I can endure whatever life throws at me. I can make the best of a bad situation and rely on my own fortitude to carry through. It will take a lot more than a Texas freeze to put me down.

Former four-foot-tall prickly pear cactus now shriveled and dead.

A BUSTED ANKLE

by Amy Baruch

Music silenced.
Transformed in a split second
Into my own wailing.

Distracted by thoughts,
The phone in my hand,
Tap, tap, tap.

While the man on the corner
Propped up on his skateboard
Saw it coming.

Splayed out on the sidewalk,
My ankle ballooned; the pain intensified.
I went out for a run,
Now I can't even walk.

Shorty, he calls himself,
The man with no legs, no ankles,
With no ID and lives outside.

He keeps me company
While I wait for my ride to the ER.
His limbs were blown off
By a car bomb planted by his mother.
He tells me, "I don't get along with my family."

As my daughter drives,
I think of Shorty,
I think of all the split seconds
I will be avoiding
At home with my leg up.
Perhaps that will save me from a real disaster.

OUR MOTHERS

From my earliest memories, I was fascinated by my mother's stories of her family's flight from the Nazis. But it was not until I took a post-retirement workshop that the thought crystallized: I would now make it my life's work to share their miraculous saga. This story is dedicated to her.

MY MOTHER'S STORY OF SURVIVAL

by Linda Aronovsky Cox

"Don't jump on my bed," she reminded me as she left me upstairs to play. "You might break something." With my older brother in kindergarten, the two younger ones napping, and me home from my half-day preschool, she knew how tempted I'd be. And she was right—the appeal was too great. I climbed up and started jumping. Bouncing higher and higher, I failed to notice that the doll carefully placed among the pillows was slowly moving to the edge, until I heard the shatter. I looked at the smashed porcelain face of my mother's beloved childhood doll, brought all the way from Belgium, one of the few treasured keepsakes from her earliest years.

She must have heard it too, or maybe she heard me cry out, because suddenly she was there, weeping. "I told you this might happen," she murmured.

I didn't realize it then, but at that moment, at the age of four, I swallowed my mother's unspeakable grief and trauma from the Holocaust. I didn't yet know her full story, but sensed that it lived deep inside her. And now it lived deep inside me.

My mother is Manné Eckstein Aronovsky. This is her story.

The World Was Changing

Born on April 8, 1933, in Antwerp, Belgium, Manné Eckstein was the second child of Baruch and Hedwig Eckstein. Her sister, Felicia

(Lizy), was five years older, and had been born in Romania before the family, along with her grandparents and aunt, immigrated to Belgium in 1929 to escape the escalating danger for Jews in Eastern Europe. They were not wealthy, but certainly comfortable. My grandfather, who was originally from Poland, had been the jeweler for the Crown Prince of Romania, and established a thriving business as a top-quality diamond setter in Antwerp.

By May 1940, the Nazi march across Europe reached Belgium. My mother saw her world changing. She could no longer attend the school she loved, play with some of her friends, or dress up and stroll with her mother and sister along the downtown streets of Brussels as they window-shopped. Only seven, she was too young to understand what was happening around her.

My grandfather recognized that the situation for Jews was becoming increasingly perilous, so in late May 1940, he led his extended family out of Brussels headed for Dunkirk on the northern coast of France. They walked the hundred miles, hoping to find their way to safety aboard a British ship that he heard would help Jews flee to England. As they carried their luggage amidst the many escaping refugees, German planes strafed the roads; and even though they jumped into the ditches for safety, many were killed.

My mother saw the dead bodies lying in the road, the fear on everyone's faces, and the chaos. She only felt safe when she held her mother's hand.

Her family survived.

So Close to Safety

On her deathbed seventy-six years later, she still smiled when she recalled the deliciously pungent aroma of food cooking. It had been permanently imprinted on her brain since the age of seven.

When they neared Dunkirk, my grandfather left the family in a safe place on the outskirts of town. My mother accompanied him into the city because she spoke French. (He only knew Yiddish.) He also felt he would evoke more sympathy holding the hand of a young child. But their timing was bad; the British army was in the midst of their mass retreat and could not take refugees. The family was so close to reaching safety in England, but now they had to return to Brussels.

On their way to rejoin the group bearing the bad news, my mother smelled food cooking. In a nearby abandoned barn, a few British soldiers were cooking their rations and other scrounged food in a metal helmet, and they generously shared their hot meal with the refugees.

The soldiers offered to help my grandfather move a cart from the back of the barn, a valuable possession to ease their trek as the strong men could pull the cart with the luggage loaded atop, along with my mother and her elderly grandfather.

On their return, at a village in northern France, they were about to join a long bread line near a bakery when my grandfather spotted two approaching planes. They ran just as a plane swooped down, dropping a bomb directly on the line of refugees waiting for food, killing everyone instantly. She remembered a small child clinging to her father's pant legs, alone, crying, looking for a mother who was no longer there. They took her to a local home for care.

My mother's family was again spared.

Final Escape

Her grandparents, aunts, uncles, and cousins refused to leave again with them. "You're young—you can start a new life in America," they said. "We're old. Nothing will happen to us. We will be safe—the Americans and the British will save us."

Two months later, after exhausting all other avenues for escape, they were back in Brussels. Her father needed a better plan. Not wanting to go to neutral Switzerland and be landlocked in Europe, he decided to head for neutral Portugal. He sold everything he could and bought small diamonds, using some to obtain false legal papers enabling them to travel, and hiding the rest in a false belt in his trousers for bribes along the way. The family could now easily pass for non-Jews, with their light-colored hair and eyes, joining my grandmother, who had already dyed her hair blond.

Before they left, my grandmother had the foresight to ship two large wicker trunks with photos, curios, bedding, and the like to "General Delivery" at their destination in Lisbon. She reasoned that if they were lucky enough to reach Portugal, they could begin again with a few of their personal possessions. If they did not survive, she thought, there was less for the Nazis to steal! (This is why, unlike most other families of survivors, we descendants have photos of our family and ancestors.)

They left two weeks later, in the summer of 1940. This time, the rest of the family decided to stay, thinking they would be safe.

All those who remained behind were soon deported and murdered in Auschwitz.

Juden, Raus!

Too young to understand the danger, my mother's travels through France felt like a grand adventure. She got to see Paris! But much to her disappointment, the Germans had closed La Tour Eiffel to visitors.

Since cars were worthless without petrol, the family traveled largely by foot across France, bringing only what they could carry. My mother was delighted to have the precious doll she had received for her seventh birthday. They either slept in the open under the stars, or if there was a farm nearby, my mother and grandmother would approach the farmhouse asking if they could sleep in the barn, and sometimes offered money for a hot meal. In larger cities, they bartered with diamonds to stay in hotel rooms.

When they arrived in northern France in late Summer of 1940, the Nazis already occupied it, so they had to make themselves invisible. They only spoke French, never Yiddish, and when they heard boots marching on the cobblestones in French towns, they pretended to window-shop, never making eye contact or showing fear, to blend in with the locals.

In southern France, they bought rail tickets, and, after boarding the train in Perpignan to cross the Pyrenees into Spain, they heard a commotion. A Nazi officer marched down the hallway, opening each compartment door, yelling "*Juden, raus!*" (Jews get out!). They looked out the window and saw many exiting the train. My grandmother said under her breath, "Nobody move. If they want us, they will have to drag us out." The Nazis, so convinced that the Jews would obey their orders, never checked anyone's papers, and the train started moving towards Spain and neutral Portugal with them still on it.

Once again, the family made it.

Safety in Neutral Portugal

Arriving in Portugal, they met other Polish Jews who had managed to escape, some of whom they knew, all desperately trying to get off the European continent. Though no one spoke Portuguese, my mother, now eight, picked it up quickly when she was hospitalized for six weeks with scarlet fever. She was proud to be the only one who could translate for the family. Portuguese officials soon sent them, along with other Polish Jews, to live in a summer resort north of Lisbon for about a year from 1940 to 1941.

Eventually, as the Nazi threat intensified, officials concluded that they needed to move as many Jews as possible out of Europe. Years before, my grandfather had arranged for American sponsorship by relatives and for a job in the diamond district in New York City, but now with stringent quotas on Polish Jews, they were not permitted to enter the United States.

In late 1941, the family was lucky enough to be selected by the American Joint Distribution Committee to go to Jamaica in the British West Indies, in a small group with 150 other Polish Jews. Somehow, miraculously, they were finally able to leave and get a little closer to America.

They departed on January 24, 1942, on the *Serpa Pinto* for the two-week journey from Lisbon to Kingston. Though the ship flew the flag of neutral Portugal, Nazi officials boarded from a U-boat, in defiance of all international laws protecting neutral countries. The Nazis checked everyone's papers, and they removed two young men without the correct papers from the ship, who were likely killed or thrown overboard soon after.

The ship that left Lisbon the day before and the one that left the day after were both sunk by German U-boats.

The *Serpa Pinto*, with all its escaping passengers, survived the voyage.

Paradise in Jamaica

The refugees were told they would receive apartments and jobs in Kingston, but that was not to be. Many felt misled when instead they were sent to a small refugee camp named Gibraltar II, built for the Jews next to a larger camp for refugees from British protectorates Gibraltar and Malta. The hard-working men were bored, eager to start their lives again and earn a living, but they were not allowed to work. Housed in the two small rooms for each family in a simple wooden WWI barracks, they had little privacy, using communal showers and eating only non-Kosher Jamaican food in a dining hall.

But my mother loved living in Jamaica. The weather was wonderful. She made new friends to play with, and her family was together. She was nearly ten and was ecstatic to return to school for the first time since second grade in Brussels, taken to the British convent school every day with the other children in a mule-drawn carriage. Already fluent in Yiddish, French, and Hebrew, she excelled in school and learned her fourth language, the Queen's English. Though she never spoke with a British accent, her English was precise, but she always counted in her first language, French. Indeed, at the very end of her life when she was in hospice, she spoke only French.

Freedom in Cuba

In the summer of 1944, after more than two years in Jamaica, friends of my grandparents arranged for the family to go to Cuba. There they could live and move about freely, and her father could resume his jewelry business. They found an apartment in Havana, and my mother attended a small public school taught in English, where she learned her fifth language, Spanish. She was now eleven, but even without years of schooling, she was placed in the eighth grade.

There were many other Jewish young people there, and soon after, she joined a Zionist club and became an avid supporter for the creation of the State of Israel. Though they recently had been refugees, my grandmother, who was highly cultured, now re-introduced my mother to symphonies, classical music, art, dance, and theater. They found a free lending library and read avidly.

Finally, in May 1946, they received visas to enter the United States, flying from Cuba to Miami, and then taking a train to New York. My mother was thirteen years old. Despite her unstable childhood and dearth of schooling, she was placed in high school and graduated soon after she turned sixteen.

They had finally reached their destination alive, exactly six years after escaping Hitler's plan to destroy the Jews.

Safe in America

She credited her family for shielding her as much as they could from the horrors of war. But how could she have escaped the trauma of what she experienced? Seemingly, though, she was left unscarred, protected by her mother, and was the darling of her father's eye.

My mother married a military officer at age nineteen, had five children in eleven years, traveled the world, and divorced at the age of forty. She then restarted her life, completed advanced degrees, and became a librarian, forever cherishing her children and her many grand- and great-grandchildren, a testament to the failure of Hitler's extermination plan.

Unlike many survivors (including her own sister), my mother often spoke publicly about her wartime experiences. She regularly gave educational presentations at schools and community events and developed Holocaust-related curricula. She was interviewed frequently in the media and by Holocaust organizations, wrote about her experiences, and openly shared her stories with me.

My mother, Manné Eckstein Aronovsky (*z"l*), Holocaust survivor, died in Columbus, Ohio, on December 17, 2016, at the age of eighty-three.

Posing with her parents and older sister, Manné holds her beloved doll. Gibraltar refugee camp, Kingston, Jamaica, circa 1942.

92 Linda Aronovsky Cox

Manné and her five children (and spouses) and seven grandchildren, proof that Hitler's plan failed. Linda and Hallie, top left. Columbus, Ohio, circa 1994.

WHEN LIFE GIVES YOU LEMONS

by Amy Baruch

DORICE AND I walked the hour's distance from the Brooklyn College campus to her family apartment in Brighton Beach. The familiar blue seltzer bottles stood vigil at the entry, and the door was open just enough that we already smelled the sweetness of chocolate and cinnamon. We balanced ourselves against the wall of the narrow hallway, hurriedly removing our shoes. I tossed my weathered Mary Janes onto the large pile of "newish" shoes. The cold tile was a relief to my blistered feet.

"Come, come," Dorice's mother said, hugging each of us in her fleshy arms. "I made babka."

She pushed us into chairs at the red Formica table, the babka and leftover apple and honey cakes already plated.

"Eat before the boys get home and inhale it."

She served us tea, then removed her flour-patched apron.

"*Oy*, so nice to sit down. Now tell me what you ladies have been up to?"

"Tell her." Dorice elbowed me.

I unraveled the layers of babka and took a large bite.

"Lucy?"

Her mother looked to Dorice.

"You wouldn't believe what she said today in economics class?"

Then she turned back to me. "And what did you say this time?"

"Well, my economics professor likes to give us *quizzies*; that's what he calls them. So, I asked him when he would be giving us *testes*."

Dorice's mother erupted in laughter. After catching her breath, she went silent.

"My dear, that took a lot of *chutzpah*.[1] I hope this doesn't cause you trouble."

---

1 Yiddish word for extreme self-confidence or audacity.

"He did ask me to leave class."

"You know, women are held to a higher standard."

"I am running an A in the class."

"Well, I hope they don't make an example of you."

I suddenly felt foolish, my eyes welling with tears.

Then Dorice's mother offered more babka. "I'm sure it'll be OK."

HER MOTHER WAVED us off to Dorice's room. "Go relax, girls. I have to get dinner going."

Dorice's bed was carefully made with a collection of pillows along the adjacent wall. Her brothers' beds, in the opposite corners, were piled high with dirty clothes and baseball mitts. I nearly tripped on a bat before collapsing onto her bed.

"You are so lucky to get a room of your own," Dorice lamented. "My brothers are such pigs. I hate having to change my clothes in the bathroom."

"I'd live at your house, with your family, if I had the choice."

"I'm sorry." She paused. "How are things?"

"My mother went for ECT² again last week."

Dorice took my hand.

"I really don't know how my dad puts up with her. I'd call him a saint if we weren't Jewish."

"Just think, once you and Mel are married, you'll be able to move out of there."

"Yeah, into his parents' basement apartment. I'm not sure how much better that'll be. Mel's mother is always getting in our business."

She offered a nod and took a long breath.

"Hey, let me show you something."

She took out a vertical strip of four photos of her and Sol.

"We took those at the new photo booth at Coney Island."

"You two are so adorable together. I think you have a keeper."

"He's planning on coming over for dinner Sunday to meet my parents."

"Well, I'm sure that'll go over way better than it did at my house."

I was startled at the sound of the kitchen timer.

"Oh, shit, I'm expected home for dinner at 5:30. It'll take me over a half hour to get to Brownsville."

2 Electroconvulsive therapy, a psychiatric treatment where a generalized seizure is electrically induced to manage refractory mental disorders.

I gave Dorice a long goodbye hug, darted into the kitchen, and kissed Dorice's mother on the cheek. She handed me a few pieces of babka wrapped neatly in a paper napkin. I ran out the door, nearly forgetting my shoes.

THE SUBWAY WAS crowded, being Friday and rush hour. I emerged from the Utica station, sweaty. The cool air felt good. I ran the eight blocks home and was panting as I came through the front door.

"Hello!"

There was no answer.

I passed the kitchen where Sonia was at the stove preparing dinner.

"Hello?"

"Huh, nice of you to come home for dinner? Your father will be home in an hour or so."

I smelled the sweetness of the stewed tomatoes and brown sugar balanced with the strong scent of cabbage.

"The stuffed cabbage smells good, Ma."

No response.

I retreated to my room. I unwrapped the babka, intentionally taking small bites to make it last, wishing I was back at Dorice's apartment. I spent the rest of the next hour staring out my window, watching the neighbor kids play stickball.

I heard the apartment door opening and closing. She was already yelling at him. And then for me to come for dinner.

MY FATHER SAID the *berakhah*[3], then lit the candles. He kissed me on the forehead, just as he had every Sabbath since I could remember.

Sonia's face looked like she'd eaten a sour lemon.

He asked me about school. I didn't dare talk about economics class.

"It's all good, Pop."

Then Sonia chimed in. "I'm not sure what good college is doing for you." She turned her back and gathered the food to put on the table.

My eyes met my father's. His face turned beet red, and his jaw clenched. I understood.

I sat quietly, stuffing myself until my stomach ached.

---

3 In Judaism, a blessing or thanksgiving often recited before the enjoyment of food or smelling a fragrance, particularly after lighting candles during the Sabbath meal.

THE LAST RAINY DAY IN SCHENECTADY

by Stephanie Cowell

THE ONLY POSSIBLE way to live any sort of real life was to get out of this suffocating and small-minded town forever, Dora thought. She had known that since she was a child. But today she was too discouraged to have plans. She could only sit listlessly on a chair by the window of their leaking house in Schenectady, looking at the icy January rain pouring down and blurring the street of other houses.

It was on the wrong side of the tracks, and she was in the wrong place in the country.

Real life was a three-hour train ride away. And she was nineteen and still here.

A few people hurried down the sidewalk with blown umbrellas. She looked at their obscured shapes. Like almost all members of her family, they were half dead and didn't know it. They earned their money in meaningless jobs, never read books or discussed ideas, never went to a real theater. One day, they would be completely dead and not even recognize it. They would still walk down the street to the bus.

But if she closed her eyes tightly this weekday morning, she could picture the skyscrapers of New York City and the rising Art Deco Empire State Building still under construction. Dora saw them again yesterday in the flickering movie house newsreel. She had leaned forward as the camera showed Fifth Avenue, the crowds, the giddy women with mid-calf skirts hurrying out of the great department stores, everyone smoking and laughing and undoubtedly talking of significant things like art and museums, things that mattered.

"Even in this year in the Great Depression," the newsman had broadcast over crackling newsreel background in the theater, which smelled of popcorn, "New York City remains the greatest city in the world where tens of thousands come to make their dreams come true and life is just swell."

Sitting by the window, Dora heard the gross sounds of their boarders as they stuffed down bread and coffee in the kitchen with her brothers talking of football and horse racing, followed by the trickle of water running in the dishwashing pan. Three boarders tramped through the living room in their bowler hats, off to work. She didn't nod at them, but remained motionless on the chair.

Her brothers once more came down the creaking stairs of this dilapidated house, which one day might collapse about their ears: Johnny, who had worked at General Electric since dropping out of school at age fourteen; and Benny, already slouched, bruised by life, a half-smoked cigarette always dangling from his lips. Her other brother Bill and her older sister Gertie had already left.

"Another day at home, Dora!" Benny called to her. "I don't know why Ma lets you. All you do is draw and read books. We're working to bring food to the table. I don't understand why she didn't take that job at the glass blowing factory, Johnny."

She saw their reflections in the wet window and thought of the factory with a shudder. She said clearly, "Because I would have died there. Our sister Sarah had to work in the five-and-ten-cent store and dropped dead."

"She died from pneumonia," Benny said.

"She died because she was brilliant and despaired of her life. I will never enter a five-and-dime, never, never."

Benny sighed gruffly. "Well, you're a case, Dora. Ma sews ten hours a day, and all you think of is books and art. You have to face it. You failed. They didn't want you. Get a job."

Johnny cleared his throat. He had been the man of the family since their father died. Now he was an office boy at General Electric. He hoped to be a salesman one day.

He fished in his deep pants pocket. "Here's a nickel, kid," he said gently. "For coffee and a donut if you're hungry later."

"Damn, you spoil her," Benny said. Both brothers left.

Dora heard the buzzing of the new electric sewing machine. Now that everyone had gone, and she was alone in the house with her mother, she took up the issue of *Vogue* magazine she had borrowed from the library. For half an hour she looked at fashion drawings and skimmed articles about New York's upper-class women, reading about how they danced until all hours of the morning wearing French gowns. She turned on the radio and, amid static, heard jazz. They're dancing there, she thought. She loved to dance.

But the train from the Schenectady station had taken other young people to New York City. She had sent her portfolio to the art school admission office in Manhattan, and it was returned with the words, "We regret." She would never forget the day the postman arrived and brought it back.

Suddenly, she was too miserable to stay alone in the cold, damp living room and wandered to the kitchen where her mother was sewing by the heat of the stove. Molly Abrahams was now in her early sixties; her heavy shoulders were bent under her floral housedress. Dora looked around at the neat piles of fabric to be sewn, and then gazed at her mother's expressionless face, dazed with guilt and longing.

She leaned against the wall and studied her own carefully manicured nails. She said in a young voice, "Tell me again why you and Papa came to America from Poland. What's so great here?"

"We weren't likely to be murdered here," said her mother. "That was a good reason. But I didn't know it would be so hard. He had to go and die on me so young. I couldn't expect more of him. From your sister Sarah, I expected great things . . . but she . . ."

Dora tidied the small stack of finished dresses. Her mother had sewn thousands for the city of Schenectady; the pile had been there since Dora remembered. But it was useless to ask more about her mother's life before she came here. Their heritage was partly Russian Jewish, marked by tall glasses of tea and her late father's songs. No nod to religion—the biggest piece of nonsense to brainwash people, her mother always said.

Molly Abrahams stopped sewing. "Listen to me, Dora, you can't go on like this. The others don't understand you. I had six children, and two with real brains, Sarah and you. The others, they try. Johnny's not bad. But *you* have the talent. You're worth the rest of them."

Dora cried, "It's no use. All I wanted to do was be an artist and the art school didn't accept me."

Hands on her knees, her mother faced Dora. "You can't give up. You have to try again. And again, and again. Listen to me. My life was made for me; I never met your father until our wedding day. I look at you and see myself, the dreamer I was. I never had the time to think of the life I wanted. I never could choose."

Dora felt something like hope deep inside her. She murmured, "I'm not like my brothers and sisters. I don't know where I came from."

"I'm not sure either," said her mother with a shrug. "They don't read. They don't think. But then I was forty-four, and a miracle happened. I had you. I don't care what the others say. You've got to try the art school once more. Do you want to break my heart?"

"Ma, someone told me. They only take two Jews a year."

"Well, maybe you'll be one of them next autumn."

"You think I could try again? How will we manage? I'm scared."

"Maybe a scholarship."

That afternoon, Dora bought two donuts, and they ate them together. She would deliver the two new dresses today for her mother, so the others would say she had done something, and pass by the five-and-ten without looking at it. Already she was planning how to create a better art portfolio. She imagined the possible school acceptance and then the train to New York. Her heart lifted. She would study, she would learn. One day she would be one of the women she had seen in the newsreel rushing down Fifth Avenue.

Dora in 1942, age thirty-two.

CODA

My mother, Dora, came to New York City during the Depression with a scholarship to Pratt Institute. Many years later, she was working for *Vogue* as an artist and was on her way to becoming one of the top fashion illustrators of the twentieth century. She did very well and bought her mother a lovely house in Schenectady.

One of Dora's fashion illustrations.

"Our mothers are our first homes, and that's why we're always trying to return to them. To know what it was like to have one place where we belonged. Where we fit." — Michele Filgate

This is part of my mother's childhood story, told in her voice. It takes place in suburban Sydney, Australia, between 1946-1951.

ABANDONED

by Karen Finch

THERE IS YELLING and screaming. Mum and Dad are both yelling at each other. I don't know what is happening, but I'm frightened. Pat is crying. I'm holding her; she feels so small, and she is shaking. I don't know where John is. I can hear sirens and more people outside yelling.

Now there are police officers at the door. Mum has got a suitcase. Where is she going? Why is she leaving? Dad's grabbing at her, but the police are holding him. She's gone. My mother has gone. She's left us. Left me, Judy.

I'M LYING IN bed, listening to the birds outside. It's time to get up. Dad is up at 5:30, so he's been gone for ages. He's a postman and they start early. I must wake up John and Pat, make breakfast and lunches, and get them to school, so I can catch the tram to my school.

Pat still cries all the time. I know she's only eight, but I wish she'd stop. Yesterday I made her sandwiches wrong, and she cried. She said that's not how Mum used to make them. It's how I remember Mum making them. They don't taste the same though. I don't know why. I want to cry too, but I can't. I can't think about Mum, or I'll cry, and I might not be able to stop. When Pat cries and it's all about Mum, I can't make it better for her, because I'm not Mum. I'm just her big sister. I'm only twelve. How can I be her mum? I can't.

PAT IS GONE. Dad said it would be better for her to live in a proper family, so he sent her to those friends of his near Melbourne. So far away for a nine-year-old to go by herself. He said she's too little to understand what happened. I'm thirteen now, and I don't understand what happened! Why won't he tell me anything? I want Mum. I want her to come home and for us to be a family again. I can't say that to Dad, though. He always gets angry when I talk about Mum.

He's working so hard. He has another job, so he's gone all day every day during the week doing the post. On Saturdays, he cleans a building somewhere. He spends all day doing the washing on Sunday. I tried to do it, but I couldn't manage the mangle[4] by myself. Aunty Dory comes on Mondays to do all the ironing while John and I are at school. Mondays are good. She makes us dinner and leaves it, and I just heat it up. On the other days, I make something with whatever Dad brings home because he's too tired to cook. Cooking is hard.

A LADY CALLED Rae has come to live with us. Dad says she's our housekeeper. But she's sleeping in the bedroom with him. She has two girls, so now I must share with them. Antonia is sixteen and Happy is fourteen. I'm fifteen now, so I'm in the middle. It's been two years since I've seen Pat.

I head home from school and as I turn the corner, I see Mum at our front gate. She's walking away toward the main road at the end of our block where there are trams to the city. I run down the street after her, but she says to go back. I keep following her, but she won't stop. She turns around and yells at me to go home. Then a tram comes, and she gets on it. She's gone . . . again.

When I get back, Dad yells at me because I'm late. I say I'm not late. I was with Mum. He yells at me again. I dash to the bedroom, crying. Antonia, Rae's older daughter, tells me they are getting a divorce, Mum and Dad. She listened at the door. Mum is never coming home, is she?

DAD AND RAE are married now. She doesn't like me. She's always telling me my hair is wrong, or my clothes, and that I'm "common."

---

4 A mangle is a hand-operated device consisting of two rollers between which wet laundry is squeezed to strip as much water as possible prior to being hung on a clothesline.

I don't know what that means. She doesn't say things like that to Antonia or Happy. Dad never says anything, even when he's there when she's awful.

My scholarship at school is finished. I want to stay at school, but Dad says he can't afford the fees. He says I must get a job. I'm only sixteen. What can I do? I find one at the Women's Hospital in Surry Hills, helping on the wards. It's all right, but it doesn't pay very much. Rae takes most of my pay for board.

Rae says I can't stay here now that I've left school. She says I have to leave. They're bringing Pat home and there's no room for me. I must find somewhere to live. I need a better job. I can't pay rent on what I earn now.

I apply for a secretary's job. I get it! Now I can find a room to rent somewhere. I can afford that, and my food and clothes. I can see Pat again.

I MEET PAT the weekend after she gets back and take her out to get ice cream. It's so good to see her. She's grown up so much. She's twelve now and going to high school. She says John's gone. Rae packed a bag and told him to get out. He's only fourteen. Where has he gone? Pat doesn't know, and I don't know where to look for him.

I AM SEVENTEEN now. I got a new job, a better one. I work as a secretary at the National Institute of Dramatic Arts. I get a staff discount if I do night classes. Everyone here speaks so nicely, like the people on the radio. I want to speak like that too. I enroll in an elocution class to learn how.

I will speak better. People here call me Judith, not Judy. It sounds so posh. They're good people. They ask me out with them, all the actors and people from the other classes too. I'm making some good friends here. They're a bit like a family.

NO-FAULT ASSURANCE

by Andrea Simon

MY MOTHER WAS forever aggrieved. I wouldn't say that she was paranoid, but she rarely took responsibility for doing anything wrong. If I didn't agree with her interpretation of events, she accused me of undermining her, a no-win situation. Although she has been dead since 2000, my sister, Barbara, reminded me of this trait during one of our phone conversations.

"Remember when we went to Grossinger's Hotel and Mommy sprayed her hair?" Barbara still used the childhood moniker even though my sister had grandchildren old enough to have children of their own.

"How can I forget?" I asked.

Since my mother's family owned a boardinghouse in New York's Catskill Mountains when she was a teenager and spent summers in our country cottage as an adult, she had never been a guest at one of the famous opulent hotels. My sister and I wanted to treat her to an all-girls Borscht Belt experience before the hotel's demise. (Grossinger's closed in 1986.) My nine-year-old daughter was delighted to join us.

When we arrived on a Friday night, the first thing my mother did was book an appointment at the hotel's beauty salon for the following morning. No matter what her financial situation, she never missed a Saturday at the hairdressers for a wash and set, so lacquered and teased that she could last the entire week without touching a comb.

The next morning as we waited for my mother to get her hair done, we didn't partake in the Simon Sez games (despite our family name); we opted for the less frenetic shuffleboard. We met my mother in the dining room and appreciated the chopped herring salad and banana cream pie among the mountains of food.

After lunch, my mother excused herself and went to the large multi-stall bathroom off the dining room. Waiting for her outside, we sat on

Adirondack chairs. With her face reddened and her teased gray hair dripping, my mother ambled toward us, emanating a strong odor of disinfectant.

"What is that horrid smell?" I asked.

"Oh, this hotel is so thoughtful," she said, wrinkling her nose. "I took a look in the mirror and admired my new setting. They had a free can of hairspray on the sink counter, and I couldn't resist giving myself a few extra spritzes."

Without explaining, we ordered my mother to stay where she was with my daughter. I dashed toward the bathroom, followed by my sister. There on the counter was an aerosol can . . . of Lysol.

We dragged my mother back into her room and shampooed her hair over the bathroom sink. By then, her nose must have overcome her poor eyesight, and she didn't question us. Through teary eyes, she insisted, "They should have had a warning on the can. How could anyone have known?"

SUCH DENIALS WERE typical of my mother. Once in an upscale Manhattan restaurant, she emerged from the ladies' room with a long trail of toilet paper glued to her foot, which, according to her, was the fault of another woman who preceded her in the stall. The towel that caught fire in my mother's hands as she turned on my stovetop was the result, she claimed, of a defective knob that I should have replaced. Her long-time habit of confiscating belts and buttons from department stores was not stealing; she deserved them due to years of inadequate sales help.

One of the most cringe-worthy of my mother's behavioral faux pas occurred on a family visit to my nephew Paul's new townhouse in Virginia. The owner of an untrained puppy, Paul warned us not to step into his backyard as the dog was using the grass as his bathroom. As Paul drove away for an errand, he reminded us again that if we go outdoors, we should take off our shoes when we come inside to protect his creamy white wall-to-wall carpet.

Already resentful of Paul's admonitions, my mother opened the front door and circled the perimeter of the house. Minutes later, I heard a tap on the sliding glass door to the kitchen. My mother slunk inside and headed directly upstairs before I realized she had left on her shoes. The phone rang, and I was momentarily distracted. Then I gasped. There was a trail of her muddy footprints on the beige kitchen tile floor leading to the white carpeted hallway and up the matching staircase. I slid open the back door to see where she had stepped, and it was clear as her size-ten footprints: a pile of fresh dog poop.

By the time my mother returned to the top of the stairs, my teenage daughter and I were on our knees with wet towels, scrubbing the brown stains from the carpet.

"Paul told you not to go into the backyard," I yelled.

"Grandma, take off your shoes. You have poop all over them," my daughter ordered.

About a half hour passed as we backtracked my mother's path and soaked her black orthopedic shoes in the sink. The footprints were lighter on the carpet, but still visible and surrounded by smudges. I anticipated fireworks. What would Paul say?

In the meantime, my mother returned to her room, put on sneakers, sidestepped down the stairs, and slipped out of the house. Shortly thereafter, we heard a car pull into the driveway, and I met Paul outside before he could see the damage to his new carpet or take a whiff of the putrid smell. Instead of outrage, he calmly pointed out that the carpet probably wouldn't have remained white much longer with his new dog around. I admired his gallantry, and we awaited my mother's return.

As the sun was setting, we worried that my mother was lost in this strange neighborhood. My husband and Paul got in their cars and drove around the area, each taking a different direction; my daughter and I went on foot. A few blocks away, we saw my mother sitting on a playground bench, her shoulders trembling.

"Mom, what are you doing here?" I asked.

"I'm not going back to *that* house," she said through tears. "Not where everyone yells at me and tells me what *not* to do."

This was not the end of the matter. What followed was a "silent" six-hour drive back to New York, followed by a few weeks of my mother not answering her phone.

Often, I thought of the traumas she had suffered to cause such unresolved hurts: surviving pogroms in Poland, coming to America as an impoverished immigrant, almost dying from diphtheria, withstanding her tyrannical rabbi father, witnessing her parents' humiliating divorce and poverty, the death of two brothers, enduring my father's monetary and moral bankruptcy. While she could be charming and reasonable, when she felt criticized, she resorted to seemingly inexplicable tirades. She had given "a piece" of her mind to so many people that I often joked that she must have used it up. In this case, I knew that the only way my mother would speak to me again would be for me to apologize. For what, I didn't know. But I did.

WHENEVER MY SISTER and I, and/or our offspring, get together and we talk about my mother, we mention one of her unseemly episodes. They always evoke a mixture of fresh embarrassment and a bizarre sense of humor.

I often picture my mother's last days as she lingered for a month in intensive care, begging for water, her chest heaving in time with the whooshes of the ventilator. My mother had been a strikingly beautiful and accomplished woman. She was articulate, well-read, and respected as a community activist. There was standing-room only at her funeral, attended by local politicians and beloved neighbors, and even those associates who endured her disdain. Why was I haunted by those horrible final hospital images? And why did my family dwell on her outlandish and often delusional behaviors?

As I get closer to my mother's age when she died, I often think about what my daughter will remember about me after I'm gone. Will she repeat her complaint that I embarrassed her by hiding behind a table and yelling "boo" when she came home from school with her friends? Will she recall that she warned me in private not to curse in front of the girls? Will she blush at my birthday-party portrayals of Madame Veronska who wore a babushka and held seances as my husband pretended to be a departed relative?

I hope she remembers that I was her friends' favorite mother. (And my mother, who donated her bedroom every Friday so the girls could watch TV late at night, was their favorite grandmother.) I hope my daughter recalls that when she criticized me, unlike my mother, I good-humoredly took the blame. Someone had to, and in my family, it was me.

TIME TRAVELING TO EAST 70TH STREET

by Stephanie Cowell

I HAVE DECIDED to go back in time to visit my mother, to talk of things that I have never managed to speak about before.

I am a novelist writing in other centuries. I time travel easily in my mind and memories. I can go where I'd like in a moment. This is a little more difficult.

I delete or move around passages when I write novels. With the change of several verbs and a paragraph or two, a sad character can become an uplifting one. In a few hours, I can redeem her. If I can do this in writing, why not in life?

It is forty years since my mother died.

I decide not to visit her last apartment, instead I return to the one on East 70th Street. I am in a hurry, so I begin my journey a few blocks from our old building. I pass the old-age home kept by nuns. I used to stalk around there for hours at night when I couldn't bear to stay home.

I nod to the old doorman, who looks at me, puzzled. But I do not choose to appear seventeen as when we lived here, but thirty-seven, the age at which I lost my mother. With raised eyebrows, he rings up. "Mrs. Mathieu, it's your daughter," he speaks into the intercom.

It is not like the Christmas when she handed me a present through the crack in the door and then slammed it shut in my face. I hear her voice saying to send me up, and already my knees feel weak. My stomach churns. Of all the places in the world I could leap in my imagination, into all those that would welcome me, I have come here.

At the front door, she looks at me suspiciously. "I've almost given up waiting for you. It's been years and years. You look well."

Now and then, I think I could have handled things better with my mother. "But what could we do?" my sister, who is nine years younger than me, said when I visited her recently. "We were kids. And what do you mean, go back? She's long gone, sweetie."

But nothing goes away for me; the past is always within me, ready to be made into stories. In the midst of it is my mother, who shadows certain characters in my books but has never appeared in one as herself. Does this past live within my sister as in me? "Don't beat yourself up about it," my sister said recently, as we looked at old photographs. "She was sick, poor woman."

So, I have not told my younger sister I am traveling today.

What mother am I visiting? For there are two distinct ones, and many variations within each. There is the malevolent drunken one who screams obscenities at me, and the rational, sober woman who draws so exquisitely and who stands in quiet awe before good art. I am careful what time I arrive because I need the sober one. And I know there is no permanent barrier between the two. Characteristics mingle.

"I need to talk to you," I say, as we sit in matching directors' chairs by the low architect's table, which is in my house today.

"So, talk," she says, raising her mug to sip her coffee. "You've been away decades. You never called." It is coffee; thank God, not a martini.

"I thought of you," I say. Emotions drag at my words. In addition to being a novelist, I am also a singer, but the self-possessed woman I am who walks on stages and sings to hundreds of people is fading; I am cowering. I must stand accountable for my life and suddenly that life means little. I have not yet achieved world fame. No matter what else I have done, there's not that, that coveted impossible place where I would be so wildly successful. She simply had to love me.

Now again, my words fumble. There is my deep craving for acceptance, to be loved for being myself. Not that I could ever allow myself to cuddle with her; she is too dangerous in her mood swings. Ever since my earliest memories, I was cautious even when she brushed my hair when I was little. I was wary of her lightest touch. I adored my father unreservedly. But he had fled long ago.

There is a long pause between us. "Well, for God's sake, speak already," she says.

I try to find my voice, that of the successful singer, the wife, the mother of two charming young boys. I have made a good life, but before her, I doubt everything. "I just want everything to be good between us." I clutch the coffee cup with both hands. "And I have to tell you things. The way you've treated me at times was despicable. I never did anything to you. I only wanted to adore you. What's the matter with you?" My voice rises shrilly . . . my lovely resonant voice trained to sing beautifully.

Her eyelids flicker dangerously. "What things?" she asks coldly. The warm apartment filled with her drawing table and art suddenly is naked winter. One look and I shrink into someone very small. I try to hold on to the thousand beautiful things of my life as I fall by them.

But I have come here. I must see it through. I must say what I've always felt.

I begin. "You always said horrible things to me and my sister that aren't true. You don't see us at all. I don't know who you're seeing or who you think we are, but you never looked at us."

I breathe a little more steadily. There.

How many years have I been afraid to say that? Would I tear down every wall of my real world saying it? But this is my dream, this is *my* time travel.

"Why, you're making that up," she says at last indignantly. "I gave you singing lessons and good schools. If you've decided to throw that away and make a mediocrity of your life, well, I always knew you would."

I have at last begun to tell her and must persist. "I understand it now. Your terrible life with your brothers and sister when they tried to squash you and destroy you. You make everyone else in your life into them. Even people you know who are good, you push away and say horrible things."

She stands. Though she is smaller and frailer than me, she holds all the power in my world. "They're all out to use me. That's all they are. That's all you are, a piece of shit. I was at the top of my field. Who are you anyway and the rest of them?"

"We're people," I say.

I sit in my chair wondering if I am worth the earth I stand on and hear the clinking of ice knocking against the glass pitcher as my mother cools the martinis. It would only get worse from here. I get up and leave.

I walk for hours.

PERHAPS IF I had traveled back another day, we might have talked about theater or something lovely. We might have laughed. But I had gone back to confront her with my truth and again, I was the enemy.

When she died, my sister and I looked up names of people to invite to the memorial service and found she had bought a new address book and eliminated those who "were only out to use her." That was just about everybody—all those interesting, kind people who came into our lives. Whole pages of the book were empty.

As I walk, sometimes crying, sometimes in rage, sometimes feeling such loss, I slowly come back into my own body and life where I have friends and two marvelous sons and an interesting background in fiction and music. And, taking this class on writing about our mothers, I form a still clearer picture of her. Born with a brilliant talent to people who mostly didn't understand her, she made enemies of everyone. She had to "pull people down" before they pulled her down.

So, I have come to this conclusion. My mother was very complicated, maybe more than most people. She was full of contradictions. I guess she had to feel she was "the top" or "the greatest" to be safe. And where did it leave the rest of us?

If I had truly dared in my adolescence and young womanhood to confront her, would she have heard? Would she have changed? I never gave up trying to find the words, but I ran away for long times and found other people who loved me with far more consistency.

MY TIME TRAVEL to her was unsuccessful. I finally said the words I wanted. I confronted her, but what I wanted her to reply was, "I'm so sorry I was so awful. I never meant it. I just can't stop fighting the world . . . I felt a lot of you were only out to use me, but you and your sister and many others weren't."

Maybe this is one of the reasons I write fiction, to make things work out, to come to some sort of end, which is healing even if often mingled with sadness. To create a world where people mostly love each other consistently.

I end my time travel and return to my apartment where my friends and family always are most lovingly welcomed and drink a little coffee and write this small story.

Stephanie and her mom, circa 1979.

THAT CONVERSATION

by Karen Finch

"I'M SORRY, DEAR. I did mean to get here on time, but I just had a few things I needed to do before I left," says Mum, handing me a bag of groceries. "Can you pop those in the fridge for me, please? Oh, and here, put my car keys in the fridge with them too, so I don't go home without them. I'll get your plants out of the car."

She never arrives at my house when she says she will. There are always things that she needs to do before she leaves home. Things that come after her routine of waking and breakfasting that include reading while she eats and adding to letters written in bits like diary entries until she signs off and posts them. I've often suggested, which never happens, that she might get up earlier on the days she's committed to be somewhere at a specific time.

But it's okay. Decades of late arrivals, accompanied by detailed descriptions, are part of who she is.

Today, we have plans to visit her friend and have lunch out. But before we leave, she's helping put in some new seedlings in the vegetable garden I'm building in the front yard.

I make coffee. I've not had mine yet, and she can always drink another one.

"I got you some bulbs too, dear. I found them in the storeroom at work the other day. They're a bit old, so we can't sell them, but who knows, they might still come up for you and I thought you'd probably have a spot to put them. Oh, and I rescued another marguerite daisy for you!"

I thank her, thinking about where I can plant them, and muse on the randomness of every garden I've ever had since she began working in garden centers. Plan as I might, there will always be something unexpected that comes through the door with her that gets added to the mix.

"Plant a daisy on my grave, will you? I'd like to always have daisies."

"What?"

"Well, I was thinking, I'd like to be someplace quiet, where you could drop by and visit, you know? A small cemetery in the country, with trees, maybe on the side of a hill. You could plant a daisy and come by occasionally for a chat."

"Oh, right? I'll see what I can manage. Anything else?"

"I don't want any fuss. No big service or anything like that. Nothing religious."

The closest my very secular mother comes to religion is a loose adherence to the Eightfold Path in Buddhism. But she doesn't want to be cremated.

"And bury me properly. Tuck me in gently."

Seventeen-year-old Jonathon walks into the kitchen in time to hear that, and recoils.

"Are you two talking about funerals again? Why are you always talking about funerals?"

"So, your mother knows what to do when I die, Jo. Not that I'm planning on that for some time yet, but your grandfather won't cope with it and your uncle doesn't want to talk about it. It'll be up to your mum."

He looks at her quizzically and says, "Yeah, well, but it's really creepy!" and heads out of the kitchen to the safety of his room.

Six months later

THE DAY MY mother dies, I'm almost out the door on my way to an opera rehearsal when I remember something I forgot to tell Mum when we were talking the previous evening. I rush back to the phone and dial quickly. It's a little later than our usual catch up, which we didn't have because we both had plans this morning. I'm surprised when Mum's friend Jan answers the phone. Something's up. They were supposed to go out together that day.

"Can you come, dear, now, please?"

Jan won't say anything else, other to repeat that I need to come as soon as possible.

I drag Jo out of bed, tell him to put on some clothes and get in the car. I explain that something has happened, and we needed to get to Mum's place as soon as possible. He sits, half asleep, silent in the passenger seat as I drive. I count the minutes, bargaining with G-d, "Let it be my father, please." He has a heart condition; it wouldn't be unexpected. But if it is him, why did Jan answer the phone?

We pull up in a flurry of gravel, splattering the trees alongside my parents' driveway. I get out of the car, lock up, and burst through the gate. Jan must have heard us and is coming along the veranda to meet me. Her face says it all: My mother is dead. She had a heart attack.

I can barely hear Jan's words as she describes the sequence of events. How Mum was sitting in her chair at the table stacking her newspaper, letters, and books, then stopping suddenly, her body seizing, and then slumping back against the cushions. Jan, who was a retired nurse, said she realized exactly what had happened, and did everything she could have done while awaiting the ambulance, but that the heart attack had been massive and would have killed Mum instantly. This makes no sense to me. No sense at all. Because my mother *can't* be dead.

I leave Jo collapsed in the outer room chair, and drop onto the floor next to Mum, where the paramedics had left her, neatly covered in a sheet, as they'd had to cut her clothes away. I sit there, and she's just so still. Her amazing pewter-toned hair is still shiny, falling softly away from her face, and her olive skin looks warm, as usual. She looks like she's sleeping. But the sheet over her chest is absolutely still.

When I go outside to see if Jo wants to come in and say goodbye, Jan's husband, Adrian, who had just arrived, asks me whether I know if Mum had any funeral plans anywhere. I tell him yes, it's all in my head. He looks at me oddly, and I tell him that Mum and I had many conversations over the years, so I know what to do. He recommends a funeral director and offers to call him.

The funeral company staff arrives faster than I expected. We're still waiting for Mum's sister, Pat, to come. No one has been able to contact my brother. I ask them if I can help. They have a large shroud with them and direct me alongside Mum's body to help wrap her before lifting her onto their stretcher. Pat rushes through the gate just as they're wheeling Mum down the veranda. The funeral people melt away quietly and allow Pat some time before loading Mum into their hearse. They drive her away.

I continue making phone calls to interstate relatives who will need to book flights and make other arrangements to get here.

The funeral director arrives two days later to discuss plans. My father is there, and my brother, Matthew, with his partner, Sharon. Jonathon, who hasn't left my side, and I have already had a meeting with Les, the chaplain from the college where I went to art school. He knew Mum well and offered to coordinate things when I rang to tell him she had died. In accordance with Mum's wishes, we've roughed out something that's not a service exactly, but that will provide a ritual for those who will need it.

"Now, did you want to discuss options for cremation or burial?" the funeral director asks.

"She wanted to be buried," I tell him, and hear the sharp hiss of breath intakes from my father and Matthew. I brace myself.

"How do you know that?" demands my brother.

Before I can snap back, Jo says, "Because they talked about funerals all the time, Mum and Nanna. She told Mum exactly what she wanted."

"Here's the thing," I say to the funeral director, "she wanted to be buried in a small cemetery in the country, on the side of a hill. And it needs to have trees. Can you do that?"

"She was that specific?"

"Oh yes. She wanted it to be somewhere peaceful, where we could visit and sit awhile."

"Well, fortunately, we're in a big council area[5] here, and a lot of it is very rural. I'll need to do some research and see what I can find for you."

Five days later

THE RAIN HAS cleared, but it's freezing on this hillside just out of Kangarilla in South Australia's Southern Vales. The funeral director has done Mum proud, even if the weather hasn't. After huge overnight storms, the clouds are still dark and turbulent, and the tops of the trees are thrashing in the wind. We'll be lucky to escape a soaking. Every time I look up, there are more people walking up the hill. The car park filled up ages ago, so they're having to park along the road outside.

Les, my chaplain friend, introduces himself and begins his service. I'm standing next to him and can feel Jonathon pressed up against my right shoulder. I see Lewis, my younger son, looking small and miserable, standing next to his father and other grandmother. Behind me, I can hear the faint hiss of oxygen coming from both my aunt and uncle's tanks.

---

[5] In Australia, the law restricts burial to cemeteries within local government areas (councils) where the dead resided, unless there is a requirement for religious purposes that they be buried in a specific cemetery outside that area.

They both have emphysema. My father is more than a little tipsy. My brother is somewhere at the back, behind me. I can feel his enmity.

This picture is all wrong. How can it be that it's my mother in the coffin resting over the open grave in front of me?

Les nods to me. It's time for me to read the eulogy I wrote. It's not a typical eulogy. Mum didn't want that. It's a string of little stories that spoke more about who she was than a chronicle of her life. As I begin to speak, there's a break in the clouds and sudden sunlight. Les told me later that the sun only peeped through twice the whole time we were there—both times when I spoke.

Each time I look up, I see a different face. My first ex-mother-in-law. Different friends from my university. My godmother, Helen, my mother's oldest, closest friend. A couple, my mother's dear friends. Members of her walking group, the poetry group, staff members from the garden center, and many faces I don't know. There must be three hundred people shivering on this hillside.

A friend of Mum's steps up beside me and says *Kaddish*[6] with me. I think Mum would forgive us that.

At the end, Les invites people to come forward and take a spade to help fill in the grave. I see someone hand one to my brother, who knocks it away and disappears through the crowd. My father is nowhere to be seen. I reach for Lewis and squeeze him to me in a hug, then give him a basket of mixed bulbs. I pull out a fat tulip bulb and put it in his hand—tulips are his favorite flower. I ask him if he'll take the basket around to people so they can plant one when the grave is full.

Some Sunday in September a year or two later

I PARK MY car and walk up the hill. Iris and daffodils wave gently in the breeze, pinpointing where Mum lies. I settle on the sandstone edge of the grave and pull out some weeds, place a pebble near the headstone—a large rock from her garden with a bronze plate fixed to it, with just her name and dates. There's a jingle of bridles and stirrups, and the thud of hoofbeats on grass. The local pony club meets in the paddock next door.

Freesias bloom under the trees around the perimeter of the cemetery. She'd like that. I did plant a daisy as Mum had asked me to, but it didn't

---

6 Prayer praising God, traditionally recited in honor of the dead.

survive the brutal summer we had the year she died. The tulips only flowered the first spring and never came up again; the winters in most of Australia aren't cold enough for tulips to survive in the ground past the first season. Only the daffodils and iris continue to thrive.

When I leave, I pick a bunch of wild freesias to take home. She'd like that too.

FINAL ABSOLUTION

by Rhonda Hunt-Del Bene

I WAS RAISED on a desolate ranch in northern Arizona, on land that has been in my family for over a century. My grandfather promised my father, Vincent, he would inherit the land if he worked the ranch for him. But my father was little more than an indentured servant, paid very little salary and given even less respect.

My parents met in college during the Great Depression. Mother found Vincent handsome with his black wavy hair and broad smile. He was the only student with a car, and his family owned land. He seemed quite the catch.

Vincent was smitten with my mother. He named his car "Josephine" after Mother's made-up middle name. The year my parents met, my mother's mother gave birth to her thirteenth child. Mother, being the oldest daughter, was expected to help care for the younger children, even while keeping up with her studies at college. Hoping to escape the poverty of her family, Mother agreed to marry Vincent. They eloped in New Mexico; Mother dropped out of college and "Josephine" carried them away to an uncertain future on the ranch.

For the first years of their marriage, my parents lived in the back bedroom of my grandparents' house. Instead of building a new home, Vincent and his father relocated the remnants of a "shotgun" style house from Penzance, a housing project for migrant workers building the railroad through that bleak part of the red Arizona desert. Mother would later tell me that the day they brought the clapboard house to the ranch, her heart sank.

Mother never had a proper home. She was raising four children in the tiny two-room house before it was enlarged. She bathed the children at my grandparents' house next door, and the family used an outhouse for the toilet, where my mother once sustained a poisonous bite from a black widow spider. It was the early 1950s.

Vincent reluctantly added rooms, including a bathroom, to the shotgun house to accommodate his growing family. But it still was not adequate. My two older sisters and I shared one large bedroom. The four boys slept in a separate building we called "the little house," without heat, air conditioning, or running water.

Mother would often say, in a voice tinged with melancholy, "Maybe I'll have a nice home when I get to Heaven."

I was the fifth living child out of the eight that she bore. Her firstborn, Vivienne Rose, was stillborn. Mother carried a lot of guilt over the death of that child. She didn't speak of Vivienne Rose often, but I overheard her tell what happened when she was fifteen. At a county fair, she had visited a gypsy fortune-teller even though her strict religion forbade it as "the work of the devil."

Mother said she sat nervously in front of the toothless old woman. The gypsy furrowed her craggy brow and waited several minutes before finally speaking. "Your firstborn will bring you much sorrow. You will have a lifetime of grief."

Vivienne Rose was delivered at nine months but never took a breath. Mother made a baby book for her, anyway. I still remember the book. Mother kept it hidden from us, but took it out occasionally and slowly leafed through the pages. We were not allowed to touch it, but I would sneak a look when she wasn't around. Perhaps I was hoping to uncover the mystery of her profound unhappiness, but the book didn't give up any secrets and Mother remained obscure.

The book had a mint green plastic cover with the texture of grosgrain. Inside was a lock of the baby's cinnamon-red hair attached to the page by a piece of yellowed Scotch tape. There was a birth certificate, which also served as the death certificate. Immortalized in the document was the ghostly imprint of two tiny feet that would never learn to walk.

My mother never made another baby book. She held on to the memory of Vivienne as if it embodied all her lost dreams and hopes. In her mind, that baby would always be perfect. She would never betray her, break her heart, or run away from home like I did when I went to Paris against her wishes.

By the time I came along, Mother's nerves were threadbare, and she was tired of mothering. I ached for her attention and felt like the forgotten child, exiled from her love, and an interloper in the family.

I was a lonely child in that tiny house filled with nine people.

AS I GREW into adolescence, our relationship became strained. We fought about everything—religion, values, lifestyles. Her strict faith required me to marry and birth lots of children, nothing more. But I bristled at the control and judgment rendered by the faith and refused to contort myself into the preconceived mold. It was then I discovered the wisdom of Ralph Waldo Emerson, "Make your own Bible." So, with that counsel, I set about doing just that, making my own way in the world.

At nineteen, I had saved enough money to live in Paris to study French at the Alliance Française. I left home and broke my mother's heart.

IN MY TWENTIES and back in the States, I was determined to climb out of poverty, so I set out on a career in commercial real estate. In Salt Lake City, one of the first projects I worked on as a leasing agent was a mixed-use commercial development owned by the controversial and high-living Saudi arms dealer, Adnan Khashoggi.

After moving to California, I negotiated a deal, on behalf of a client, with Donald Trump's New Jersey casino people for a location in the Spotlight 29 Casino in the Palm Springs desert. Trump had licensed the casino from the Twenty-Nine Palms Band of Mission Indians, and of course, he renamed it "Trump 29."

At the first meeting with the casino group, I walked into the conference room and there, above the table, hung a giant portrait of Trump. Such portraits were later part of the lawsuit against the Trump Foundation as they were illegally financed by the so-called charity.

But on that day, I stared at the painting, then asked one of the New Jersey tough guys, "Am I required to genuflect in front of Trump's portrait?"

Without missing a beat, Mr. New Jersey replied, "Only the first time." That was the icebreaker. From then on, we got along well, and I negotiated a favorable deal for my client.

I navigated well in the world of the mega rich. I visited their private jets and yachts, where dining rooms were lined with African mahogany, exotic fur-covered barstools, and golden bathroom sink fixtures. I'm sure neither Mr. Trump nor Mr. Khashoggi had ever seen, or even heard of, a shotgun house.

I was proud of my accomplishments. As a girl I had to wear flip-flops to church because my parents couldn't afford proper shoes, but now, without support or mentoring, I had found a way to success. I had written my own

Bible. However, at some point, I quit telling my mother about my career. Once I had shown her the slick brochure for the Khashoggi development and her only response was, "Are you sure you know what you're doing?"

My career had no value in her eyes.

IN CALIFORNIA, I met my husband, Enzo. At age thirty-six, I married him at the Ritz Carlton Resort, on a cliff overlooking the Pacific Ocean in Laguna Niguel. Surprisingly, my parents attended, but my father declined to walk me down the aisle.

My husband is Italian-American with dual citizenship. He inspired me to study Italian. Realizing I had a deep passion and ability for it, I pursued a degree. In the past ten years, I have spent months traveling, including living and studying in Italy. There I found the culture, the history, and the language I most identify with. I found my own Holy Land . . . and peace.

AS MY MOTHER lay dying in her home, each of the children was led into her bedroom, one by one. We were instructed that we could only stay a few minutes, but Mother wanted me to read to her from a book she was trying to finish about Eve and her choice in the Garden of Eden. I was intrigued that it was important for her to finish *this* book before she died. According to the narrative, Eve played an important role in the Garden. There was no undercurrent of apology or blame, as in most literature about Eve. Instead, it treated her choice to eat the fruit from the tree of life as a pivotal role in the future of humankind.

I continued reading aloud even when it seemed Mother was asleep. At one point, she slowly opened her eyes and looked directly into mine, as if seeing me for the first time. Her cornflower-blue eyes were wider and more intense than I had remembered, perhaps from the drugs administered to steel her against the pain or from the anticipation of her own death, when she would be reunited with her loved ones.

"I think you are a lot like Eve," Mother said. "You are smart and spunky. And I think you lived your life exactly right."

I was stunned. After the years of bickering and estrangement, I couldn't remember ever receiving a compliment such as this from her. Even though her breathing was labored, she continued. "Thank you for all the beauty you brought into my life." She closed her eyes again, and I let her sleep.

Waiting in the kitchen, I looked around. The walls had always been, and were still, painted a mint green, her favorite color—the same color as the baby book. This room was so familiar, and yet something palpable had changed.

My mind wandered back to her final words. What did she mean by *beauty*? Was she referring to our shared love of books and words? We both loved the fine arts and classical music, while most around us listened to country and western. Did she really think I had lived my life exactly right?

I WAS IN Italy when my mother died. By the time I arrived for the funeral, her body was prepared for the viewing. The coffin was draped with a heavy veil. Against protocol, I drew back the cloth to look at her face. She was as pale as a magnolia blossom, immobile, cold. *This was not my mother in the coffin.* The round face in life was now cut at angles, ravaged by cancer and the inability to eat for months. Even in death, she was obscure.

My mother was buried in the family cemetery on a hill overlooking our ranch in the red Arizona desert. All my family members will be buried here. But I will not.

In the Tuscan countryside, there is a castle, Villa Castrum, built a thousand years ago by a Tuscan nobleman. This is where I stay and where my soul resides. High on a hillside overlooking Villa Castrum, my ashes will be scattered in a *venticello* (gentle breeze), mingling with the soil, and becoming a part of my Holy Land as it carries on for another thousand years.

The evening after my mother's burial, I returned to the cemetery. From her grave, I could see the shotgun house and I murmured, "How unfair that you died in the house you so despised." The sky was aflame with one of Arizona's famous sunsets. An October breeze rearranged the clouds into the form of angel wings, and I whispered, "Fly on angel's wings, my dear mother. Fly to your heaven. And I hope you find your perfect home there."

Standing over her grave, I felt cold and empty, like there was something more to be said. As I laid a rose on the mound of freshly turned earth, I thought, "Now there will be no final absolution or unconditional acceptance." But after a moment, I recalled my mother's last words to me: that I was "smart and spunky" and that I had lived my life "exactly right." In those words, I found a modicum of peace.

From cemetery hill, I took in the vast expanse of the ranch that has been in my family for over a century. My soul resided in Europe, and yet there was an inexplicable tie to this hardscrabble land where my father worked his fingers to the bone to provide for his family. I remembered how three years earlier I had stood over the casket of this compassionate, principled man, looking at his rough, calloused hands folded in reverence upon his chest. At that moment, I was overcome with gratitude for my parents' sacrifices, for the work ethic and character traits they instilled in me. Under my breath, I whispered, "Forgive me."

Perhaps I will leave a few of my ashes to be scattered here as well.

LITERARY LIFE

A TEACHABLE MOMENT

by Kathleen M. Rodgers

"MOM, WOULD YOU read this book so we can talk about it? It's really good."

I looked up from my writing. The moment was decades ago, a brief exchange I had with my oldest son.

Hesitating, Thomas handed me the book, aware he'd interrupted my work.

Back then, I was struggling to complete my first novel. The three-hundred typed pages of onion skin stuffed in a bottom drawer didn't count. I was working on a new novel. A novel I believed I had a chance to finish and get traditionally published.

From the time my two sons were toddlers, they'd grab a book and bring it to me so we could enjoy it together. I'd stop whatever I was doing to grant them their wishes. Books and my sons have been some of my greatest teachers. Sensing this was a teachable moment—and I was the student—I stopped what I was doing.

Curious, I glanced at the title and then up at Thomas's eager little boy face. "*A Wrinkle in Time,* huh? What's it about?"

Thomas burbled with excitement. "Mom, you just have to read it. See, there's these three lady characters you're going to love: Mrs. Who, Mrs. Whatsit, and Mrs. Which."

And so began my journey into the magical world of Madeleine L'Engle. After I finished reading *A Wrinkle in Time*, I checked out her memoir, *A Circle of Quiet,* from the downtown Fort Worth Library. Although it's been years since I read it, I can recall that warm surge of hope I felt as I lost myself in her story where she talked about the numerous rejections she faced until *A Wrinkle in Time* found a good home and became an international bestseller.

Back in those days, I hungered for acceptance when it came to my writing. But I didn't just hunger for publication, I hungered for a writing community. I tried for years to find a writing group, but I could never find a good fit. Sometimes it's all about trust.

As I read Madeleine's words, I felt like I'd found a friend. And I kept reminding myself that if a famous writer like Madeleine L'Engle could be rejected but still believe in her work, then an unknown like me could keep trying to hone my craft and persevere.

TODAY, AS I work on my sixth novel, I'm grateful for all the writers I've met over the years. Not long ago, I discovered a book, *A Circle of Friends: Remembering Madeleine L'Engle*, a collection of stories and poems edited by Katherine Kirkpatrick, an editor, author of several books, and a member of my writing group, Lady Bunch. As I read each entry, especially the ones written by Katherine and two other Lady Bunch members, Stephanie Cowell and Jane Mylum Gardner, I got weepy as I realized these writers not only knew the acclaimed author, but they considered Madeleine a teacher, mentor, and friend.

At the back of *A Circle of Friends,* I discovered that Andrea Simon, our intrepid leader of Lady Bunch, had a hand in putting the collection together. Simply put, to be in the same company of such accomplished writers fills me with a joy that's hard to explain.

I am thankful that I took the writing class that morphed into the Lady Bunch and includes Amy, Karen, Linda, and Rhonda, four more talented writers and fearless women I'm proud to call friends. As we've all journeyed together since the fall of 2020, I'm grateful to be included in a circle of writers where trust goes hand in hand with getting the story down.

Years ago, my son Thomas trusted me with his heart when he asked me to read a book that he loved. I have him to thank for introducing me to Madeleine L'Engle's work. Recently, I was invited to a birthday party for Thomas's young niece, an avid reader who loves books. Imagine the joy in my heart as I watched this child unwrap the gift I brought, a new hardcover edition of *A Wrinkle in Time*. As she held the book in her hand and grinned at me, I explained how this novel was one of her Uncle Thomas's favorite books as a kid. And like Thomas decades ago, I burbled with excitement. "See, there's these three lady characters you're going to love: Mrs. Who, Mrs. Whatsit, and Mrs. Which."

Thomas's teachable moment had come full circle.

Lithograph of Kathleen by her son Thomas, entitled "Motherly Secrets," 2011.

BOOK PARTIES À LA AUDREY KIRKPATRICK

by Katherine Kirkpatrick

STOP BY THE autographing party at the local museum's bookshop to purchase my latest historical tearjerker, and then continue up the road a half mile, past the duck pond, through lush woods to the home of my parents, Audrey and Dale Kirkpatrick, and a gourmet meal. Anyone from the Three Villages (Stony Brook, Setauket, Old Field) of Long Island, New York, might be there: the tennis players, the bridge players, the bank teller, my mother's hairdresser, the neighbors, teachers my siblings and I had, and people my parents knew through the Presbyterian church, puppetry, charities, real estate, Dad's travel agency, or his heart surgeries.

It didn't matter if anyone read my books, not really, because I had the great satisfaction of selling a hundred hardcovers in an hour. Even better, the sense of celebration that filled the air was as palpable as the aroma of sautéed onions and mushrooms. My father had a joyful personality and loved having people over, and my mother had the creativity and organizational skills to carry out their ideas.

The Kirkpatricks knew how to throw a party. Chicken cacciatore, anyone? Genoese seafood risotto? Champagne cocktail? In the octagonal living room decorated with carved screens from India and statuary salvaged from bombed cathedrals in Europe, in swiveling chairs with colorful satin pillows, around a central coffee table and a low-hanging lamp (my paternal grandmother once said, "The house looks like a Turkish brothel"—how did she know?), the drinks and the conversations flowed.

This was how my parents celebrated the publications of my first three books in the mid-to-late 1990s, when I was in my early- and mid-thirties, before I married, moved coasts to Seattle, and had children.

I evoke the memories of those dinners with some frequency. My parents are gone now, their house long since sold. I've now published nine books, both fiction and nonfiction, but celebrating new publications hasn't been accompanied by the same joyous feeling as when my mother was alive. Audrey Kirkpatrick, who cut sun-dried tomatoes into strips, shredded prosciutto, and grated Parmesan cheese for all my parties (and who studied literature at Cornell University under Vladimir Nabokov), served as my biggest supporter and publicist. Not only did she feed a hundred people for dinner, but she also kept boxes of my books in her closet so she could give them out to friends. In the case of *Redcoats and Petticoats,* she purchased the cover art for a thousand dollars, framed it beautifully, and displayed it in a prominent place on a wall that led from the living room to the bathroom. After my parents died, I lost my support and childhood home.

More recently, I've had small parties in bookstores in Seattle, where I've invited my local friends and provided food. New projects haven't gone unacknowledged. An older friend, Jean, now deceased, acted as a mom figure and came to one of my book signings and bought multiple copies. My husband and sometimes my children have attended signings. Every once in a rare while I've been invited to fancy publishers' parties at the American Library Association, once in New York City's Rainbow Room in an upper floor of a skyscraper, and once in an even more phenomenal meeting space at the top of Seattle's Space Needle. Yet my mother's generous dinner parties far surpassed those other occasions with a feeling of joyousness and community.

No one in my life will ever lavish such time, attention, and money on me when my book is published.

What I had, I will never have again.

BUT WAIT. THERE is an extreme fallacy in this way of thinking. The experience of publishing my ninth book, *The Art of William Sidney Mount: Long Island People of Color on Canvas* (coauthored with Vivian Nicholson-Mueller) proves to me that time and spirit are expansive. I can always go home, because on some deep psychological level, I never left it in the first place. Audrey Kirkpatrick, in some very real yet intangible way, is still slicing onions and mincing garlic for me, as ever.

You see, I wrote about my mother's favorite American painter, William Sidney Mount. Through connections in my past, I chanced upon some little-known research involving this nineteenth-century Three Village artist that I knew would make a worthwhile book. And I knew of a publisher who would take it on. Some book projects carry a certain charming energy, where external circumstances easily fall into place; my Mount book was such a project.

I didn't consciously set out to write the book for my mother. The awareness of what I was doing was gradual as I held conversations with her in my mind. I told her about long-ago people in Stony Brook's past who were portrayed in the paintings she knew well. I taught her about a multicultural approach to historical research that would not have occurred to her and, in the past, wouldn't have occurred to me, either. I'm evolving; and astonishingly, so is she, in my imaginings. It's a phrase we hear often that our departed loved ones "live on in us." I used to think of those words in a figurative sense. I now take them literally. With my latest publication, Mom and I move into the future together, along with a host of true-life characters featured in Mount's art.

I've saved some of the most delightful details of this story for last. The Long Island Museum in Stony Brook, a half mile away from where I grew up, owns the majority of the artwork featured in my book. The old building converted into the museum's gift shop is the same place where my first book signings took place more than a quarter of a century ago. It now carries my new book. Closed for some years due to disrepair and COVID-related challenges, the gift shop reopened; and the person in charge of the renovation happens to be the daughter of one of my parents' friends from their tennis and beach club days.

Life came full circle, to be sure. It isn't hard to imagine Audrey Kirkpatrick in that shop, smartly dressed in a tailored designer suit and heels, bragging to her local friends at a book signing, and afterward welcoming them to dinner at the house. I close my eyes and can smell the aromas. Chicken cacciatore, anyone? Genoese seafood risotto? Champagne cocktail?

GHOSTLY IMAGINGS

by Andrea Simon

AS I SCAN this month's prompt selections, I stop momentarily at the "ghost" suggestion and smugly dismiss it, my skeptical hackles activated to their fullest. I pride myself on the supremacy of empirical proof for otherworldly claims: séance visitations, UFO landings, psychic predictions, and mysterious nightly noises emanating behind walls. I don't believe in the supernatural, spirits, demons, disembodied souls, amulets, four-leaf clovers, or crystal balls. Yet, I am also someone who often writes about the dead, obsessing about reconstructing ancestral footsteps. Perhaps it isn't that I don't believe in ghosts in the literal interpretation, but that I don't believe in the concept of spectral beings inhabiting spaces of the living. For me, the definition of "ghosts" needs an upgrade.

As a child, I had an immediate affinity for my maternal grandmother, Masha, who immigrated to America with nine children in 1923. In her distinct broken English, overladen with Yiddish, Polish, and Russian fragments, she would regale me with stories about her native village, Volchin, in what is now present-day Belarus. One of her most vivid stories was during a pogrom when she was an adolescent. Masha's mother smeared her daughter's face and hair with flour so that she could pass as an old woman and escape rape from the Cossacks.

Although most of her extended family also immigrated to America, Masha often spoke of her brother Iser Midler, who, along with his wife and three daughters, stayed behind in Volchin and disappeared during the Holocaust, their fates unknown. Later, the family learned that Nazis slaughtered nearly four hundred village Jews during a September 1942 massacre in Volchin.

IN 1997, I joined a Jewish group from Arizona on a mission to Eastern Europe. We would be the first Americans to visit some of the former

Soviet territories, including Belarus. During this momentous trip, I met an Israeli contingent in Brest, who were former residents or descendants of Volchin. During a tumultuous rainstorm, I accompanied this group to my family's ancestral village and stopped at the "nicest" house, a white brick, one-story structure abutting a former orchard and now occupied by a priest.

It was clear from my Israeli guide, Shmuel, a former Volchiner, that this house, though certainly renovated over the years, was the Midler's residence, the home of my great-uncle and his family, the place of his bicycle repair/sewing machine shop, the "nicest" in the Jewish section that was selected by the Germans to be their headquarters. In front of the house, I closed my eyes several times and felt riveted to the spot. I heard my grandmother's disembodied voice urging me on. There was a distinct cacophony in my head, at first attributed to the thunder of the storm. But I could make out female voices, and I swore they were the good-natured chattering of my cousins Ida, Sala, and Ester, three beautiful and talented girls who had everything to live for.

The district police officer led us to the open field at the end of the village, where the Jews were massacred. At one point, while standing at the summit of the hill, I slipped and slid down, loosening my camera strap from my shoulder. Lying on the lumpy ground, I felt the pulsing earth and heard the wails of half-dead bodies trying to find a resting place.

The next day, we joined other Jewish mourners in the forest area called Brona Gora, between Minsk and Brest, where an estimated fifty thousand regional Jews were killed in eight huge pits. As we stood in the forest and listened to *Kaddish*, I pictured skeletal beings playing hide-and-seek, their emaciated bodies no wider than the thin barks of the birch trees. These spectral beings were searching for solace.

WHEN I RETURNED to America, I researched these massacres and found the three-paragraph testimony of the only recorded survivor of Brona Gora, a twelve-year-old girl named Esfir Manevich, who lay naked in the pit, crawled out, and escaped into the woods. The story of her miraculous survival stayed with me for many years, even after I had written about my trip and subsequent research, published in 2002 as *Bashert: A Granddaughter's Holocaust Quest*.

Although I wrote other books, more literary and novelistic, Esfir's story continued to haunt me. How could a girl, not even thirteen, ever have a normal life after such an experience? She seemed to nudge me with her terror; she screamed in my nightmares. Like my grandmother, Masha, Esfir begged me to tell her story. So, in 2016, I published *Esfir Is Alive*, a novelized interpretation of her remarkable story. I reimagined Esfir's hometown of Kobrin. Of course, it made sense that she would go to Brest and meet my Volchin cousin, Ida, who attended that city's Tarbut school. In my new world, Ida became Esfir's mentor and invited her to Volchin, where she befriended the entire Midler family.

Finally, the voices of the dead came to life as only true *landsmen* could. Though I often worried that the real Esfir would emerge from the shadows and berate me for making up her life, including her experiences in the massacre, I silently hoped she would be happy that I resurrected my precious relatives in a respectful and realistic manner.

Through the years, I did not restrict my work to reconstructing the dead. I fictionalized real-life characters from my childhood and interspersed them with made-up friends and more dramatic plots. Often, I took my real-life counterparts and set them free to discover an entirely different path, but one true to their new nature as recombinant beings.

Now, I often recall an incident from my youth and then stop mid-sentence. Did this really happen to me? I wonder. Or did I make this up? Like an often-viewed photograph that becomes the remembered experience, my literary world often supplants reality. Who is to say that this new worldview isn't more satisfying, more cathartic? Isn't it the job of a writer to reconstruct her past, make it more palatable and explicable?

I used to laugh at my childhood friend Joanie, who read my first autobiographical novel and wrote in the margins, "I remember this." When I pointed out that she noted these comments on purely fictional passages, she insisted that the only childhood she remembered was the one I wrote. But who is to say that I was alone in the rendering? Now, I know better. I had an army of volunteers, the ghosts of the past.

LONGING TO BE READ

by Kathleen M. Rodgers

A YOUNG MAN with curly hair and a round cherub face approaches and thrusts a book at me. "Why haven't you read my book?" he demands. His voice is full of rage, his expression one of disgust and disappointment.

I've just climbed out of a car, and I'm preparing to close the door and step on the curb when he appears out of nowhere. His accusation blindsides me.

Glancing around, I'm filled with fear that he's confronting me in some parking lot somewhere. "You wrote a book?" I stammer, wracking my brain, trying to remember him.

Before he can respond, I bolt upright in bed, realizing I've been dreaming.

His question and the anger on his face leaves me rattled. "Who are you?" I mouth in the dark, careful not to wake my husband as I stumble out of bed to get a drink of water and check on my dogs. Sometimes a sleeping dog all curled up can offer comfort when no one else can. After I pad back to bed, I toss and turn, haunted by this young writer's question.

The next morning, as I let the dogs out and make coffee, I try to make sense of the dream. Later, after analyzing it, I feel an enormous sense of relief that I'm finally admitting what has been building up inside of me for a long time: guilt.

Guilt that I've bought too many books since the pandemic hit and many of them have gone unread. Books are stacking up around me, overflowing into every room in my house. This normally isn't an issue, except that many of these latest books I've ordered are penned by colleagues and friends. In some cases, I've promised to write reviews and post online about their books. There are the occasional books sent as gifts from other authors or the advanced reader copies from publishers and authors seeking endorsements. Offering an endorsement is a huge honor and a responsibility I take seriously. Because these books come with a reading deadline, they usually take top priority if I choose to offer my recommendation. They go to the top of my list. Then there's the dozen or so books I'm reading for research on my current work in progress.

So, here's my confession. Although I've been writing professionally for over four decades, not only am I a *slow* writer, but I am an even *slower* reader. I'm always trying to juggle reading and writing on the same day, but I don't multitask well. Someone or something always gets hurt.

When the pandemic hit, I was preparing to launch my fourth novel. Like so many other authors in the same position, we regrouped and learned new skills and ways to get the word out about our books. I am grateful for every person who offered to help with my book release.

Years ago, I coined this saying: "When we elevate others, we elevate ourselves. Let's all go be elevators." I'm a big proponent of supporting other authors, and not just authors I know. But somewhere between unveiling my fourth novel and supporting so many fellow authors, my "elevator" came crashing down. My physical and emotional motors burned out. It didn't happen overnight.

I've been chugging along, lifting others up for years. In between, I promoted myself. When I shined the spotlight on someone else, I recognized their hard work and helped spread the word to potential readers. But I've been forced to reexamine my motives: If I promote others, am I hoping they'll return the favor someday? And if they don't? It's the expectation that others will read my work or help advertise it that can leave me disappointed. By admitting this hard truth, I am giving it wings, setting it free, so I can be happy again.

HAVING TOO MANY books isn't a problem but a *privilege*. I get that. I'm grateful I was able to help many authors, even if all I did was buy their books. But here's where I've run into trouble. After months of not being able to write for many reasons, I'm back at work on my next novel. I call this process building a book. And now that I'm immersed in research, I'm overwhelmed with the prospect of facing down another story calling to be told. Characters and scenes spin unwritten in my head, nagging me to get them down before they fly into oblivion. When I'm actively writing, I pour my entire self into the project. I often joke that I don't so much write books as worry them into being.

Back to the young man in my dream. I finally figured out who he is. He's every writer who's had the courage to sit down and attempt to create a story out of thin air. He's every person with a dream to write a book with the simple longing *to be read.*

MY LIFE AS A BIBLIOPHILE

by Linda Aronovsky Cox

WHAT IS IT about print books that make them so desirable? Even with the advent of e-books, when forecasters predicted they would destroy demand for physical books, print sales have actually increased (much like the cinema after the birth of television). My love of printed books is a sensory experience. Holding and feeling them is deeply satisfying, and takes me back to my earliest days, when books served as both comfort and distraction. I cannot imagine what would happen if I was stranded without a book, which is why I always carry something to read, just in case.

I became a book lover as a toddler. In one of my father's few good parenting moments, he sat me at age three-and-a-half on one knee and my year-older brother on the other, as we looked at a workbook called *Teach Me to Read*, an early educational primer with a teaching method clearly before its time. The words were simple—cat, hat, bat, and so on. I quickly figured it out and was off and running on my lifelong journey with books. I never stopped.

The library became the sanctuary from my chaotic and painful family life. In the second and third grades, our classroom lessons required students to take turns reading aloud from the Dick and Jane primers. My teacher, Mrs. Oliver, noticed that I would become bored and fidgety as I finished a whole chapter while the first child was stumbling over the first paragraph, so during lessons, she sent me to the school "library" (a converted closet with shelves on four walls and a small table in the center) to read alone during class reading time. It was heavenly.

Saturdays were for family visits to the library on the military base in Columbus, Ohio, where we lived. I would make a stack as high as I could carry, usually the maximum allowable, knowing that I would finish them long before the next Saturday came around. In later elementary school years, the beautiful stately old Carnegie library in the small town of Charlevoix, Michigan, my father's next military assignment, had the children's section in the lower level down a broad formal marble staircase. I could walk there and joyfully spend hours reading every weekend. The hush of silence from the shelves covering every wall, the marble floors, the thick mahogany tables and chairs enveloped and soothed me, as I felt swaddled by the silence.

I continued reading prolifically through my teens (many classics) and on through adulthood. During this time, my mother became a librarian, living our shared booklover's dream job. Eventually, it should come as no surprise that I married a writer who was a booklover. His specialty was Texas history, and he had many thousands of volumes in his personal library. I began learning the finer points of evaluating books and soon collected on my own. We sought bookstores everywhere we traveled; the fun of collecting pre-internet was in the search.

Though I have scaled back after my last downsizing move, I still collect titles by children of Holocaust survivors (my mother was a survivor), historical treatises and biographies of Jews in Texas and the West (most began as peddlers), early tomes on child-rearing (eighteenth and nineteenth centuries, most written by men of course), as well as books by authors Maurice Sendak, especially the earliest, and Elie Wiesel, many signed.

For many years, my husband and I operated a home-based, used, and rare book business. Now divorced, I am running the business myself, selling fine collectible and scarce titles—mostly history, technical, and the unusual—online and at an antique mall booth.

Books have always taken a prominent place in my life. I delight in spending an inordinate amount of time reading book reviews and perusing lists of newly released and recommended books to include in my "want-to-read" list on an online site. There, I also delineate categories for each so I can search and find the perfect one to read next. I've coordinated my book club for more than ten years, regularly visit bookstores, and, before I can post a book for sale, I spend way too much time studying and enjoying it. And of course, all this is in addition to actually sitting down—or in my preferred position, lying down—with a great book.

The unfortunate truth is, as one of my T-shirts confirms, "So many books, so little time."

BOOK COLLECTING BASICS

Why collect? Unless you're a minimalist, or prescribe to the guidance of tidying expert Marie Kondo, many people are inclined to collect something like stamps, doilies, or pottery. For me, it is cobalt blue glass and antique baby bottles.

Collecting books is in a unique category, because it can be done on any budget, any subject, any author, or with countless other characteristics. Just pick an area or subject that interests you most, keeping in mind the more specific, the more satisfying the discovery.

Books can beautify your home and show you to be part of the intellectual literati. It's a little-known secret by non-bibliophiles that booklovers often smugly judge those who have no books in their homes.

Collectible books will likely increase in value over time, but not like precious metals or gems. That is not the best reason to buy a book, unless you come across a very valuable one for a cheap price.

The best reason to buy a book is because you love it or it adds to your collection, not for the investment value. But if you find a book that is in better condition than the one you own, you may want to trade up to increase the overall quality—and value—of your collection.

Determining Value

Like everything else, supply and demand dictate the relative value of books. The internet has altered this factor—what may have been considered scarce can now be easily found, a bonanza for collectors, not helpful for sellers. In general, the fewer copies of a particular book, the more valuable it is. This includes an edition—if only later editions are available, the first one is worth more. The same holds true for the other factors—dust jacket, signature, condition, etc.

• **Condition**. Consider the real estate principle of "location, location, location." For books, the most important factor is "condition, condition, condition." If the dust jacket is absent, or torn, stained, or damaged, the value drops considerably. Other important factors are the binding and spine, especially if broken or loose. Watch out for general wear, such as frayed edges, stains, bumped corners, ink marks, or writing. Water on books destroys them just like acid. The more pristine the condition, the closer it looks to a new book, the more valuable. (An exception: for highly scarce books, condition is less significant.)

• **Age**. Many think that age determines value. In some cases, it does, but not necessarily. Many old books are in poor condition, and scarcity and other factors are significant. Of note: old family bibles are usually worth little, except as history to pass on to descendants.

• **Edition**. This is what makes a book more valuable as a collectible. Out-of-print books are harder to find, so are more valuable. First editions and first printings are ideal; you can identify that on the reverse of the title page. Since the 1950s, publishers have included a row of numbers, with the lowest number indicating the edition, but there are many exceptions.

• **Dust jacket**. If a book was issued with a dust jacket, it should be intact. Readers often discard the dust jacket—a huge no-no for collecting. If there is a price printed on the upper right corner of the front flap jacket, it should not be clipped; that can affect condition.

• **Signature**. Books signed by the author usually have higher value, sometimes much higher, with some exceptions. The most valuable signature is of the author alone, or with added date and location. Personal inscriptions can detract from the value unless the recipient is well known. If the author signs many books, the signature becomes common and will not enhance the value.

Caring for Books

Books, like most things and people, do best in a climate-controlled environment. This means not in a garage or a non-climate-controlled storage unit. Bugs can be a problem, as well as mold and mildew, paper damage, dust, and dirt. They also do best upright on a bookshelf, not flat. If you must store them flat, put heavier books on the bottom and lighter ones on top.

Handle them gently, like the prized objects they are. Never use them as a coaster; there is nothing worse than seeing a coffee ring on the dust jacket of a great book! Don't place them upside down when open; that could weaken or break the spine. And as tempting as it is, don't dog ear a page to mark your place. Always use a bookmark, index card, scrap of paper, or anything thin and flat. And *never* highlight, underline, or write in ink in any book unless it is one you don't care about. No bookplates, no inked signatures. If you want to claim ownership or mark a page or passage, lightly use a pencil so it can be erased by a new owner.

If it is a special book, or one you seriously value, don't lend it to anyone. Borrowed books are notoriously lost, misplaced, or forgotten. Years later, when you look for your special copy, you may remember your long-forgotten friend who never returned it, and now it is gone forever.

Linda and her mother, a school librarian, select titles at a used bookstore in Columbus, Ohio, circa 1990.

SINGULAR
PASSIONS

ALL THE HORSES I NEVER OWNED

by Karen Finch

I DON'T REMEMBER the first time I was put on a horse. I know it was on the ten-acre block where my godmother, Helen, and her family lived, and the horse would have been Trinket, a small, bay Australian Stock Horse with a white blaze down her face. I'd have been a preschooler, because family photos show that Helen and her husband, Ian, bought that land in the foothills of the Blue Mountains and erected a kit house on it when I was around two, and the horses followed soon after.

My brother and I, and Helen's four children, all learned to ride on Trinket. She was that sensible, bomb-proof animal any horsey family needed for their kids. We took her onto parts of the property we were permitted to access on weekends and school holidays, and the six of us ran wild. We built camps in the patch of natural bush, creating a corral for her by tying lengths of hay bale twine from bush to bush, and she'd patiently stay put within them while we cooked sausages over a small campfire.

Over the years, there were more horses, including those bought specifically for Helen's children as they became involved in different equestrian exploits. I wanted one of my very own. But we lived in a crowded inner-city suburb of Sydney, two hours by car from Helen's place. Over time, my brother ceased to ride, so Trinket became available for me whenever we were there, and I could accompany Helen's son Richard, who was the same age as me, on rides off the property, the only rule being to shut any gates.

The last ride I ever had there, Richard woke me very early, and we went out just as it was getting light. By then, the city was encroaching on those ten-acre blocks, and before long, we were clattering through paved streets with houses popping up here and there. Little children in pajamas flew to the front windows of the houses to watch us go past.

In a conversation with my mother decades later, I discovered that when Helen and Ian bought that land, my parents could have done the same thing. Mum wanted my brother and me to have that semi-rural upbringing. I could have had horses. But my very urban father refused, which is how we came to be in a little single-fronted cottage in a suburb very close to the center of the city.

When I was nine and a half, my father moved us halfway across the country, chasing a job with the Australian National Railways, based in a small country town on the edge of the desert in South Australia. As we adjusted to small town living, I discovered girls at school who had horses. Maybe now I could have one. Only, it didn't happen.

To "cure" me of my horse craze, Mum organized my first job when I was eleven, as a stable hand at a professional stable of Standardbreds—trotters, as they're known in Australia. "Going to the trots" was a popular evening event. Attendees watched these horses harnessed to lightweight buggies or "bikes" as they were known within racing circles, pacing around a dirt track. I didn't earn money, as it wasn't legal to have a paid job until age fifteen. Mum thought that I'd get over horses and riding if all I could do was mucking out stables, feeding, and grooming.

I loved it. One of the trainers who came midweek, when I was there after school, took me out on the two-seater training bike and taught me to drive. It was a whole new experience—everything between horse and driver communicated via the connection between hands and the bit in the horse's mouth.

I never gave up pestering Mum for a horse. Eventually, she handed me over to a local property owner who had horses he hired out for one- and two-hour rides. Soon, I was riding there every weekend, and given the run of the property on my own. The land was largely flat, but with sudden, treacherous dips to dry creek beds filled with red sand, lined with tobacco bushes. The ubiquitous saltbush concealed them, so as I wound my way on narrow sandy trails, suddenly there'd be nothing in front of me, and what happened next depended on which one of the two mares I usually rode that day. Dark bay Jedda was reasonably sensible and would prop then take me safely down into the creek bed, then up the other side back onto firm ground. The chestnut Flight was a whole other story and would usually take a fast right or left—whichever way headed back to the yards where there was hay—and then bolt.

Around the time I was sixteen, a friend popped up with a two-year-old, just-broken gelding that needed someone to ride him regularly. Somehow, I got Mum to agree to let that be me. He came with a bridle, but no saddle so we had to track down one I could borrow indefinitely. He lived in a yard in a nearby village, and one of the conditions of me having him on free lease[7] was that I got myself there and back. So, I was on my bike every day after school, riding the six or so kilometers there to catch him, saddle up, and ride, then rub him down, feed him, and cycle back, all before it got dark. Thing was, my mother, who fussed so much about our safety, mine particularly, and who'd have been horrified by the adventures I had on that mad, young horse, was perfectly okay for me to ride my bike on the shoulder of the main highway alongside all the semi-trailers and road trains! One of the many dichotomies I never figured out about her parenting.

When I finished high school, we left town for the capital city so I could go to the university. I didn't want that to happen. I wanted to go to the big city by myself and live in one of the uni (university) colleges with my schoolmates. But, no, Mum packed us up and moved the whole family.

RIDING WAS A very sometimes activity during those uni years. I didn't know anyone who had horses, and it was too expensive at places in the local hills. After dropping out and getting married, I had to fight my husband to get my first Siamese cat, so a horse was completely out of the question. He also discouraged me from riding with other people, as he felt we should do everything together and he didn't ride.

I married again, some years after the failure of my first marriage. To his credit, despite being deathly scared, my second husband went with me for a two-hour ride in the Adelaide Hills—the range that rings the city. Half an hour in, he could hardly breathe. It turned out that he was very allergic to horses. Thankfully, someone else on the ride had antidotes, so he survived to tell the tale, but it was his first and last ride with me.

On a camping trip a few months later, we became friendly with the couple in an adjacent pup tent, and discovered they used a nearby riding venue that offered lots of different rides, including their most popular, the

7 Free lease is a term used in Australia when you have the use of a horse, and are responsible for all costs, but don't own the animal.

pub ride. So, I left my husband, son, and dog and headed off with them. The ride took us up through the coastal bush to a small town where we tied up and ventured into the pub for a drink before mounting up and heading back along the beach, a truly magical experience.

MY TRACK RECORD with relationships wasn't great. My second marriage also failed, so it was just me, my two sons, two cats, and a big dog, on a limited income and a precarious rental existence. I was doing contract work for the local opera company, studying at art school, and working at one of the garden centers with my mother one day a week. After the initial rough period of working out custody and visitation arrangements, we settled on weekdays for the boys with me and weekends with my ex. This left me alone every weekend.

My good friend Judith had bought thirty acres in the hills about half an hour's drive from my home. She was breeding miniature horses, and with the dog, I'd often spend weekends with her, doing horse stuff, albeit on a small scale.

Horace, one of Judith's neighbors, was an old stockman who bred Australian Stock Horses[8]. He had a second acreage across the road from Judith's where he kept some of his breeding stock. In true country tradition, he made himself known to Judith when she arrived in the area, and soon became a friend. He would stand next to me leaning on a fence, and watch Judith working with some of her mares, shaking his head and saying he just couldn't quite see the point of a horse that couldn't be ridden. Then in his seventies, he was still competing in stock horse championships, and winning. I watched him in one show doing barrel races, and no other competitor could come close to his time.

He turned up one day riding his big chestnut gelding and leading a pretty bay mare, all saddled up, inviting us for a ride. We took turns on the mare, Judith heading off first. At that point, I'd not ridden for some years, and waited impatiently for them to come back. Judith was glowing when they stopped in front of me and handed me Missy's reins. I mounted and settled into the comfort of the big stock saddle, then realized I needed to lengthen my stirrups, so got down again to do that. As I remounted, I saw Horace nodding to himself as he watched me. Then we set off. Judith's

---

8 An Australian breed created for the purpose of working with livestock.

property was surrounded by plantation pine forests. We headed up the trails, and he grilled me about my riding history. When I said I'd been taught by a stockman as a child, he nodded again, saying that with my seat, that was very clear.

The next weekend, Judith was with Horace, who took me back to his place. Waiting for me was a small, light-gray mare with black points. Her name was Jasmine, an Arab Cross Stock Horse, one of Horace's surplus horses. She was a very different ride from Missy. Smaller, narrower, very skittish and nervy underneath me. She'd always been the "extra" horse and had never bonded consistently with anyone. But she was lovely. And so it was arranged. I just needed to get my hands on some tack, and I could have her as a free lease, and Judith could have Missy. It was a few weeks before we were organized, and with a bit of shuffling, I started out with Horace to meet Judith and Missy halfway across the forest to take her home.

I renamed her Jazz after that ride back to Judith's. It had rained the day before and there were still puddles everywhere. She would *not* set foot in them and danced her way around them sideways, through shrubs, and across fallen logs. There was no way she'd get her feet wet! She also didn't like losing sight of the others and led me roaring up a hill after them—and before I knew what was happening, we took off over a whole fence worth of fallen logs that were across the path. Apparently, I had a jumper!

It took some months for her to trust that I'd keep coming back. In the meantime, she did everything she could to get me off, and I had a few spectacular falls. But I learned to stick on fast, no matter what she did. Then there was a time during the school holidays when I was able to pack up and head to the farm for a few days. Arriving late in the day, I wandered over to the gate to the paddock where the mares lived. They were about halfway across, grazing, and swung their heads up to look when they sensed the movement, then went back to the grass. In a magical second take, Jazz's head came back up and she stared hard at me, knickered, and came to the gate. It was the first time she'd ever done that. Suddenly, I was her person. No one else could catch her except me. She'd follow Missy and a biscuit of lucerne hay through a gate if Judith moved them to another paddock but wouldn't be touched.

Always skittish when tied to be groomed and saddled, she also hated having her feet picked up to be cleaned. She never would walk through a puddle and shied at trees, which was tricky when we were riding in a forest!

I was counting my pennies by then, thinking about how I could scrape together enough money to buy her. The asking price was five hundred dollars, which was a small fortune on my budget at the time. She felt like mine by then, but it was going to take time to accumulate the funds.

Then one day, we had them both tied up to a new rail, getting ready to tack up and go for a ride. It was in an open space at the top of the driveway, so I'd tied Jazz extra firmly. Missy started, and Jazz freaked out, rearing back and pulling the railing off the uprights. Before I could grab the rope, she'd turned and was tearing down the driveway with the railing still attached, bumping along beside her. I tore after her because the gate was open. She swung left when she got to the gate, onto the road, and I made it to the end of the driveway just in time to see the rail hit a bump in the road, flick up, and hit her head. She went down like a stone. I could hear Judith shouting at me to stop. But Jazz was lying still on the road, blood oozing from a wound on her temple, very dead.

I fell to my knees next to her, trying to pick up her head, but it was too heavy to move. Then Judith's arms were around me, pulling me back up, saying we had to go and call Horace, so he could drive the tractor around to get her off the road before a car came along and hit her. He came, we went back and helped attach the ropes, and then walked behind as she was pulled back up to the yards. Judith sent me home then, knowing that Mum was with the boys waiting for me. I drove back home, numb and still in shock.

To this day, I mourn Jazz, and the only comfort is knowing that for that short time she had a bond with me and knew she was loved, something she'd never had in her twelve years of life.

Horace offered me another of his horses, Topaz, and slowly, life on the farm readjusted. While she had her own quirks, Topaz was a much more sensible horse than Jazz, and there were some good times for Judith and me, riding in the forest and getting more involved in the local equine community. However, my time at Judith's farm came to an abrupt end when my ex took a job across the country, and I suddenly had the boys full time. I could no longer spend my weekends there. We did try, a few times, with all three of us, but although they'd visited many times, and seen foals and calves born, being up there while I rode was a whole other situation. Part of the deal for me having a horse there, too, had been my contribution to the farm work, and I couldn't do that either.

THE BOYS ARE both adults now. The riding I've done since has been very occasional with my current partner, which has had its amusing side. He's a jock. He was an elite hockey player and came very close to being an Olympic cyclist. He plays all kinds of sports, is a surf swimmer, and very affectionately calls me his "nerd." Then came the weekend he said we should do something I'd like, and that I should look up somewhere to ride out of Sydney. Early one morning, we headed north to a wonderful property that offered physical activities, including riding. When I rang to do the booking, I said my partner was a complete novice, and I could ride.

It was a funny morning. My horse was delightful. For the first time, my partner saw me doing something athletic at a level that was far above him. He still tells people I ride like the famed title character from Banjo Paterson's *The Man from the Snowy River*. We talk about owning land one day, in which case there will probably be horses.

Victorian High Country, out of Dinner Plain, Australia, 2001.

HAIR

by Amy Baruch

They sneered at her,
And then whispered,
"What a terrible mother,
Giving a perm to such a young child!"
Coarse, thick ringlets.
Worn in Mickey Mouse pigtails,
For my kindergarten photo.

Then cut so short,
No longer curls.
Instead, a halo of frizz.
"Excuse me, son,"
I hear in the grocery line.

Second grade, Mrs. Drier's class,
Picture Day lady offers to "pick" my hair.
The photos come back,
And I look like a Conehead from *Saturday Night Live*.
The ever-so-popular Farrah Fawcett hairdo,
Feathered and bouncy,
Is never an option.

Years of growing it out,
Slow as a tree.
Then Mom's hairdresser
Cut, cut, cut all the curls.
I wait until I am home to cry.
I swear no more five-dollar haircuts.

No hairdressers in my neighborhood
Know how to cut or style.
Years then, cutting my hair.
Trifold mirror in my parents' bathroom
So I can see.
Cut, cut, until it's one length,
Except for bangs,
When wet, shade my eyes.

Frozen curls on winter days,
Defrosting during first-period class.
Dripping on the back of my shirt,
Leaving a faint water stain.

I am in my twenties,
Sitting in a restaurant,
I see a hairstylist across the street,
Wielding a scissor,
And comb,
Like an artist with a paintbrush.
Finally, a person who knows my hair.

It's all about the cut and the products:
The right shampoo and conditioner,
Leave-in and leave-out,
Styling gel and hairspray.
I must wash it once,
Maybe twice,
Definitely not every day.

I lack the patience
To style my voluminous hair.
I wrap it safely away in a bun,
And tame the lion.

Worn back too tight for too long,
And pregnancy leaves me a blank patch
Shaped like a V.
Fear I will start looking like Gallagher,
Who juggles bowling balls and axes.
Plenty of hair to patch it.
The donor site at the base of my scalp,
Itches when I need to wash my hair.

Fifty-five now,
Worn completely hidden from view
Under my head covering for work,
Required for COVID-19.

Will I hold on to this hair?
Few old women look good with long hair,
Except maybe Georgia O'Keeffe.
Or will I lose it to illness,
Like cancer treatment?
And then even my transplant line will be visible.
I remind myself to exercise,
Eat a plant-based diet,
And meditate.

My daughter's hair.
Perfect curls.
Soft and manageable.
Her hair journey is, let's say, less kinky.

MY GRANDMOTHER'S BLANKET

by Jane Mylum Gardner

I ARRIVE IN North Carolina at three months old, wrapped tightly in layers of softness, my cloth diapers dry, my parents numb from the trip crossing the mountains of Tennessee and Kentucky. Carried into the house in a basket that now sits on the back porch, I am handed over to my North Carolina grandmother, who has never seen me. Lord knows, she cradles me in her arms, holds me close to her chest, and takes me into her heart with her breath. We are one and I am hers, a belonging I have not known. I found her and she has claimed me. No one, not even my mother, will ever get me back again.

My mind meanders . . . I remember sitting in a wooden highchair at Grandmother's table, close to the coal-burning stove that warmed my back and the kitchen. Nearby, I hear the clatter of dishes being washed in a porcelain sink and the tea kettle gently simmering steam from the coal stove. I fall asleep and someone carries me into a dark bedroom and lays me in the middle of a featherbed. A sheet and blanket tuck me in tightly. The voices continue, the meaning of words escape me. The pulled-down shade keeps the chilly night air outside. Still, the windowsill rattles. The house sings to me.

Decades pass and the voices are long absent from my life, but their kindness remains alive in me. I have lived a long life, longer than even my grandmother lived. On this frigid winter evening, I lie in bed rubbing one cold foot against the other, a nightly ritual. I recall how Grandmother would wrap her tiny feet on top of mine, trying to share the warmth. On particularly frigid nights, she would fill up a rubber hot-water bottle, wrap it in a towel, and put it under the covers at the foot of the bed. After she turned off the bedside light, we snuggled under a quilt she made during World War II, a few years before I was born.

The blanket was not beautiful, but it was functional, the best she could do. The itchy navy, black, gray, and brown six-inch squares were samples made for tailors who fashioned fine men's suits. God knows how any man could possibly have wanted a suit made from this wool. But while the men were away fighting, the tailors' unneeded samples fell into my grandmother's hands. Night after night, she painstakingly stitched one square to another, until she completed a blanket large enough to cover her double bed. It was Grandmother's contribution to the war effort. Her anxieties turned into something positive and tangible.

The pattern, outlined with a running stitch of red embroidery thread, looked pretty enough, but the wool scratched me terribly. I much preferred the other softer side, a polished cotton with pink and red roses. Under Grandmother's blanket, we fell asleep in our little flannel nightgowns, spooning. We fit perfectly. Grandma wasn't much taller than me. In my sleep, I felt protected.

Now, as I press one foot against the other under the same woolen blanket, I remember this blanket was hers, ours. In the dark night, those memories spooning with my grandmother comfort me. The very blanket that kept me warm as a child now handsomely covers my bed.

My mother had safely buried this work of art in her hope chest. Forgotten, this out-of-fashion blanket has not been used for years. Its story had not been shared. I am the holder of that story, the last remaining part of the spoon.

Out of the darkness come my memories. Like the running stitches on the blanket, I weave the words together whispered by my tiny grandmother. I am the keeper of images too precious to forget. But there is no one in my family to tell. So, I tuck the stories inside the hope chest and pray someone years from now finds my grandmother's blanket and treasures its warmth.

Prompt: Bring two seemingly unrelated items together in an essay, i.e., a book and a statue.

PAS DE DEUX

by Rhonda Hunt-Del Bene

THE WATER BELOW us is impossibly blue—a tint of azure found only in French Renaissance paintings. Seamlessly, like a *pas de deux*,[9] there is no distinction between the sea and the sky. Tonight, its placid appearance belies how fervidly it beckons us to leave our perch high above the Mediterranean and return to its warm, healing waters, where we had languidly spent the afternoon.

An estival breeze disturbs the calm evening air, and it seems we are riding in the endless blue, like proud gods in chariots surveying the mortals below. I'm sitting with my husband, Enzo, in a restaurant on the rooftop terrace of our boutique hotel located in the forest of La Colle-sur-Loup, just outside of Saint-Paul-de-Vence, a medieval hilltop town on the French Riviera. This region of France is befittingly called the Côte d'Azur. We are five kilometers from the sea, but the height of the terrace and the slope of the terrain toward the coast below affords an unobstructed view.

On our table sit two items—a brightly painted porcelain cat and a small, antique book with gilded pages, but no title. I acquired the cat in Saint-Paul-de-Vence. He is a capricious piece of art created by the artist Soizick de la Bruguière for the French porcelain company, Limoges. Famous for its china, Limoges pieces are typically staid and utilitarian. My cat, however, is not. He is avant-garde, like his namesake, Louis XIV, the Sun King who ruled France from 1643 until his death in 1715—exactly 72 years, 110 days. However, I call my cat *Louis Cat-orze*, a play on words of the French pronunciation of Louis XIV.

---

9 French, meaning "step of two." In ballet, a *pas de deux* is a duet in which the dancers, typically a male and a female, perform steps together and is characteristic of classical ballets such as *Sleeping Beauty*, *Swan Lake*, and *Giselle*. It can also mean a close relationship between two people or things.

The azure color of my cat mimics the sky. He is adorned with an eclectic array of hearts, scrolls, and stripes in varying shades of violet and orange, with scattered dots and swirls of gold in raised relief. The artist signed his name, first name only, in a dramatic flourish of golden letters. *Soizick!*

Years later, I am delighted to discover a photo of Monsieur de la Bruguière's color palette and learn that Louis's blue is no. 20. The orange, which I call "tabby orange," is no. 36. His violet hue is no. 14, and perfectly aligns with his name, Louis XIV, and the color purple long associated with royalty.

I PURCHASED THE book on the table two weeks earlier in Paris—thanks to a fortuitous mistake. Enzo and I became lost on our way to an obscure chapel that was not clearly marked on the map. We saw a young couple loading kids and soccer equipment into an SUV. Using my best French, rusty from years of non-use, I approached them to ask directions. The father seemed to know how to guide us, but his young son stepped in to correct him.

Eager to practice his English, the boy asked, "Where do you come from?"

"California," I replied.

"Oh, I love California!"

"Have you been there?"

"No, but someday I will go."

He gave us directions, and we were on our way. As the SUV pulled past us, the kids leaned out the windows, waving and yelling, "*Vive la California!*"

In a full, throaty voice, I responded, "*Vive la France!*"

We wound up at the Seine River, across from the cathedral of Notre-Dame de Paris. This was not our destination. We were still lost. The directions were not correct.

But what luck had befallen us!

ALONG THIS STRETCH of the *Rive Gauche* (Left Bank), the Parisian *bouquinistes* have been allowed to ply their trade since the fifteenth century. *Bouquinistes* are sellers of used and antiquarian books. We leafed through piles of items, ranging from old movie magazines with Elvis on the cover to vintage postcards. I came across a postcard depicting a girl's face. It was a detail taken from a French painting, and the girl looked startlingly like Enzo's niece!

I held up the card and asked, "Who does this look like?"

"Gina! It looks exactly like Gina!"

I bought the card, and we moved on.

We came to a stall displaying the insignia of a lizard looking at a sword, an emblem that indicates integrity and professionalism in the rare book trade. The lizard symbolizes the booksellers, always in search of the sun to sell their wares. The sword represents the aspiration of used book dealers to become recognized as "professional booksellers," a noble status bestowed on its members who were then granted the right to carry a sword.

Among the stacks, I found a small book. It was bound in an olive-green silk that was much like the texture of a fine grosgrain ribbon. The cover was gold-leafed with flowers and vines, and the pages were gilded. The edges of the spine were frayed from many years of opening and closing. The book had no title or date of publication, most likely because its circulation was limited to a select group.

Our *bouquiniste* explained that the book is called an *Heures* (hours), a collection of prayers, hymns, and masses that would have been used by a nun. It was widely popular in the later Middle Ages, emerging around the thirteenth century. I carefully leafed through the pages and saw that it was written mostly in French, with some Latin, and contained devotionals to be said at the canonical hours in honor of the Virgin Mary. This copy was very old, but the thin, pink ribbon that served as a bookmark still clung tenuously to the spine. The pages with engraved drawings had fine tissue paper protecting their images, but some were discolored with mildew.

Without haggling, I paid the twenty euros and quickly stuffed the tiny book into my purse, all the while imagining a devout nun clutching it fervently, sending her prayers heavenward, perhaps from Notre-Dame, which we could see from the stall.

THAT NIGHT IN the south of France, I had brought *Louis Cat-orze* to our restaurant to show to our waiter, Ludovico. The previous evening, he had told me where to find the Limoges shop, and I wanted to present my fine acquisition. Also, I had hoped he could interpret some of the archaic French words that I did not recognize in the book of *Heures*. However, we learned he was an Italian from Genoa and could not help me. But we *did* discuss how Louis's cerulean color matched the cloudless sky, prompting *Ludovico da Genova* to tell us of a popular Italian song, "*Volare.*" In a striking tenor voice, he belted out some opening lyrics, "*Mi dipingevo le mani e la facia di blu.*"

In the song, an artist dreams he is flying, and in the blue sky he paints his face and hands blue. Although the song is Napoletana, Ludovico told us that it was inspired by a Marc Chagall painting.

I thought it sounded more like a Picasso, but I didn't argue because the lyrics intertwined seamlessly with the azure theme of the evening.

THAT WAS TWENTY years ago, in 2002. Two seemingly unrelated items came together—a cat named Louis XIV and a nun's prayer book— and created a memory that, like a *pas de deux*, still carries me back to the Côte d'Azur.

Some might call Louis and the book *souvenirs*—a word "borrowed" from French and used in English to mean a "cheap, disposable knickknack." To me, they are much more than that. Louis sits in a prominent place on a shelf among my beloved books. The book of *Heures* is next to him. At times, to practice my rusty French, I recite some of the devotionals. Wearing white cotton archival gloves, I gently turn the brittle pages and read the prayers out loud. I can't help but wonder about the nuns who might have turned these same pages. Were they sending up their prayers from Notre-Dame? Or maybe from a tiny convent in Avignon during the thirteenth century when the Catholic Church had three popes at the same time, two of them living in the south of France? I will never know.

In French, the term *se souvenir* is a reflexive verb that means "to remember something." So now Louis and the book are tangible reminders of a time that is now incorporeal—a warm summer evening, floating above the Mediterranean Sea, in the south of France. And I treasure every moment leading to their discoveries. If I could, I would preserve each one perfectly in a hologram, to be replayed again and again, exactly as they unfolded. But, alas, the human memory is fallible.

Louis XIV, the cat.

"Heures" — Book of Prayers (with "Gina" postcard from Paris *bouquiniste).*

SHE'S COME UNDONE:
A Poem about Liberation

by Kathleen M. Rodgers

Stepping out of the pool
wearing nothing but a dare,
she looks around.
No roofers in sight,
only the neighbor's cat
curled under the mimosa
and a gecko doing pushups on the fence.
She crosses her arms in front of her,
covering herself like a shield.
It's the Pilgrim in her, you know.
Then slowly, she drops the facade,
lifts her arms wide,
and does breaststrokes in the air.
The stars aren't even out,
high noon howls at her back
as she glides this way and that,
barefoot in the sun,
pirouetting in grass that's still green
until the scarecrows come out.
A hawk flies overhead,
his high-pitched keeee calling her
to join him.
She takes off across the yard
and decades fall behind her,
shedding the years until she is five
and running through sprinklers.

Diving into the blue,
she torpedoes through the water
propelled by an energy
she hasn't felt in years.
When she comes up for air,
she spots two lily pads of cloth
floating nearby . . . the discarded suit.
Flipping on her back,
the buzz of a light plane catches her attention.
And she laughs at the moment
when she defied convention.

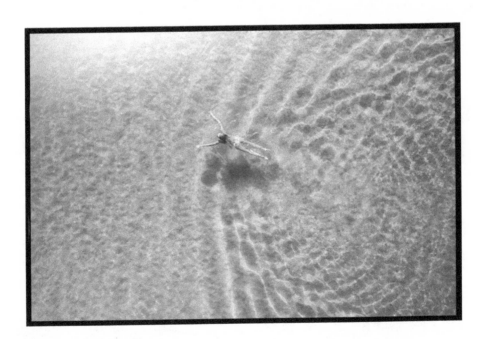

PEOPLE AND
PLACES

Prompt: Study a photograph from a family album.

MY STEP-GRANDFATHER, THE SPY

by Andrea Simon

THE OFFICIAL WEDDING picture of my grandmother Masha and her third husband, Michel, is black and white with a scalloped white border, a convenient wallet size apparently popular in 1950 pioneering Israel. I have two copies of this photo, but only one has a Yiddish inscription on the back. In brown ink, the handwriting is neatly horizontal, not the usual loopy, uneven script that Masha used, sprinkling in her unique combinations of English, Yiddish, Russian, and Polish. I assume this writing is from Michel, properly introducing himself to Masha's huge, scattered American family.

A David Niven lookalike, Michel sports a dark, finely trimmed mustache to go with his slicked back hair and shaved cleft chin. He is impeccably dressed in a white shirt, black bow tie, and dark suit, complete with a triangular white handkerchief in his breast pocket. Standing, he is a distinguished contrast to my seated grandmother, whose metallic and braceleted long gloves clutch a huge bouquet of light-colored roses. Her thick salt-and-pepper hair is squashed under a black netted hat; her long dress is a light brocade. She looks matronly and serious. I can see that Michel, at forty-five, is younger than Masha at fifty-seven.

In the album that Masha created of her married life with Michel, there are other photos of their Tel Aviv wedding, as guests crowd under the *chuppah*, facing two religious men holding a scroll. I don't recognize anyone in the photos except for the Israelis Luba and Boris (identified on the back), who had introduced Masha to Michel in his nightclub, six weeks before the big day. As later photos reveal, my grandparents' age differences seemed to disappear as Michel gained weight and Masha cut her hair in a modern short style, often posing in her mink cap and matching stole, looking regal alongside Michel's undernourished family in Riga, Latvia.

What always surprised me about Masha's wedding was that she had one at all. My glamorous grandmother had already lived a difficult and adventurous life as the wife of an orthodox rabbi in Poland (my biological grandfather), a mother and stepmother to nine children escaping pogroms and arriving in Ellis Island, a boardinghouse proprietress in the Catskill Mountains, a nurse who married her first patient, a rich widow who traveled around the world via ocean liners and jet planes. Now Masha had another life, and this one would be far from me.

At the time of Masha's marriage to Michel, I was only five, but I remember hearing the phone ring several times late at night and a lot of screaming at my mother's end. The next day, relatives crowded into our tiny tenement apartment in Brooklyn to discuss the shocking news. The question on everyone's lips was: "How could she marry him?" He was, they assumed, after her money and surely wanted an entrée to the United States. My uncles called my grandmother in Israel and tried to talk her into an annulment; they ordered her to protect her money from this Lothario. Even in my child's mind, I suspected that all these elderly relatives were wrong. Michel, whomever he really was, would be fortunate to be with my grandmother. He must have been smitten.

THERE'S SO MUCH to say about the mysterious Michel Hiro, whose name was shortened. After their marriage, the couple moved to West Berlin so Michel could collect reparations from the government for being a concentration camp survivor (so the family thought). By the time I was old enough to know more about Michel, he owned and managed a nightclub called Chez Nous, drawing on his experiences from such establishments in Paris and Tel Aviv, which featured entertainment by female impersonators (as they were called then). At the club, he wined and dined famous movie stars, and the cabaret setting was featured in films. He later established an upscale Russian restaurant called the Troika. By then, Masha was accepted as his wife, twisting Yiddish into German, even though she traveled back and forth between Berlin and Brooklyn, each locale pulling her in opposite emotional directions. When Masha would be away from Michel for a while, she would receive a bouquet of red roses with a note saying, "I miss you." She would then go to her phonograph and play their song, Edith Piaf's "La Vie en Rose" and respond by telegram, "Darlink, I'm coming."

Through the years, Masha and Michel entertained in their posh apartment on Düsseldorfer Strasse, decorated with bold colored pillows and green leaf wallpaper. Michel had become a popular entrepreneur, overworked with sleepless nights and a demanding clientele. He befriended everyone, including former Nazis and Soviet gangsters; all customers were family.

During this time, Masha wrote long letters and placed several phone calls to the State Department and other immigration officials (not to mention monetary bribes) to sponsor a visa for her husband to come to the states. It always failed, and we never knew why. As my mother's sister was married to a once-physicist at Los Alamos and knew the Rosenbergs, there were those in my family who blamed Communist paranoia for preventing Michel's acceptance. And there were others who swore that Michel not only hobnobbed with unsavory characters, but excelled in clandestine wartime pursuits. With the recommendation of some lawyer, Masha got a Jewish divorce, called a *get*, in 1956, hoping that Michel could get a visa on his own. Claiming they later remarried, she maintained her transcontinental arrangement until she was in her late seventies and on her way to dementia. She died in a nursing home in 1982, close to ninety years old.

In his Berlin years, Michel was a successful businessman and spent lavishly. If he was initially after my grandmother's money, he seemed to have no further need as his resources flourished. Masha accompanied Michel on several trips to his family in Riga. They dragged suitcases filled with medical supplies for his physician sister and clothes and food for the relatives. Perhaps Michel needed a "mother figure" in Masha or was using her to cover up some dubious sexuality. I prefer to believe they had a love affair in their own way.

I GOT TO test out my theory in 1964, when my grandmother sent my mother and me tickets to West Berlin. At eighteen, I had traveled nowhere further than New Jersey, so I was delighted to meet my new step-grandfather. Their one-bedroom apartment was stylish, but small. My mother slept on the couch, and I squeezed into an alcove off the kitchen, more like a closet.

I felt sophisticated, and a little "naughty," when I sidestepped into the narrow smokey corridors in his cabaret, Chez Nous. At the beginning of the show, Michel appeared on the tiny stage and said, "*Mein Damen und Herren,*" the audience suddenly shushed while Michel, in a sonorous voice, introduced a chorus of gorgeous, bleached-blond singers with contralto voices, who were really men. Amidst the flutter of yellow- and turquoise-dyed ostrich feathers, Michel, in his black suit, commanded us to pay attention—and have a great time.

Michel brought us to the home of one of his best friends, a German judge who, according to my mother, was undoubtedly an ex-Nazi. When my mother dared to question his whereabouts during the war, Michel's face reddened. In a barrage of German, Michel rose and walked over to the glass-tiered cart with a pitcher of water. He must have apologized for my loose-tongued American mother and tried to change the topic by encouraging the judge's son to take me to a disco. To my humiliation, Michel handed the boy a wad of marks to cover our expenses.

On another occasion, Michel dragged me to his customer's clothing studio, and insisted on buying me several high-fashion dresses and jackets, too sophisticated to wear in Brooklyn. Although I protested, I didn't want to appear ungrateful and couldn't resist Michel's insistent— and, for me, embarrassing—offerings. My grandmother didn't begrudge my gifts, but she was not happy with Michel's obsessive spending on employees and other occasional acquaintances. I heard their constant squabbles as she interrogated him; he would invariably leave, slamming the front door, mumbling incomprehensible Russian.

Yet, Michel was no patsy. He also wanted to show us a truthful picture of the geopolitical situation and invited a non-German friend to drive my mother and me down the dangerous streets of East Berlin past Checkpoint Charlie. From our car, we got a view of destruction that few in the controlled West saw. And when we got back to my grandparents' apartment, Michel and Masha were in the dining nook, sitting at a marble bistro table for two, sipping champagne flutes and gazing at each other like newlyweds.

IN 2015, I received a letter from the United States Department of State regarding my inquiries of one, "Michael Hirschkowitz." It transferred my requests to the National Archives and Records Administration, which eventually sent me a bulky file on Michel. It contained barely readable photocopies of correspondences from 1943 to 1957, including extracts from the British MI6 and American intelligence services referring to various aliases assumed to be Michel. Only one testimony was from someone who claimed to know Michel; and it was smudged and difficult to read.

A top-secret report from 1946 said he was an adviser on Polish/ Russian refugee problems in France and took orders "directly from Moscow." In a report from 1947, his assumed alias had a different DOB and hometown. On behalf of the Germans, he had supposedly "amassed a fortune" as the owner of an export company invested in land and hotels in Paris and the south of France. He fled to Spain with his wife where he smuggled jewels. The report said that between 1941 and 1945, he possibly held Monégasque, Argentine, Cuban, and Puerto Rican passports. In 1945, this "Michel" was found dead in Spain, though his identity was not substantiated.

A "secret" report from 1956 identified him as a collaborator with Germans during the war, penetrating the French Resistance, as well as a Soviet Army Captain, a Soviet agent, and a holder of an Israeli diplomatic passport (and undoubtedly an Israeli spy). I could imagine him in a description of him as a black marketeer. Just how he strapped gold watches and necklaces around my grandmother's midriff when she returned to America, I can attest. I remember one phrase from another page that called him "elegantly dressed." This one must have been him.

The last report referenced his "apparent" connection to David Greenglass, the brother of Ethel Rosenberg. It included the name of my uncle, the physicist, and my grandmother's name and Brooklyn address. This was the only report that had information I could corroborate. The others were vague and filled with inconsistencies. If even half of these accusations were true, then Michel was a master of subterfuge. Like Forrest Gump, he was in the thick of the action of his day—multi-national espionage activities before and during World War II. Or more like the brilliant imposter Frank Abagnale, Jr., played by Leonardo DiCaprio in *Catch Me if You Can.*

That he was a chameleon who took advantage of black markets to survive, that he was an opportunist who worked the systems to his benefit, could all be possible. That he was probably nonpolitical and non-nationalistic, that he spoke numerous languages and could function in a multitude of intellectual and royal circles, I can believe.

The last I heard, Michel died in a nursing home in Germany. This, too, was never verified. However, I will never know the truth.

Wedding photo, Tel Aviv, 1950.

Masha and Michel, 1962.

MY THREE FATHERS

by Stephanie Cowell

I AM THE result of a two-week love affair between a man who was mostly gay and my glamorous mother. As the story goes, it being World War II, he left her bed in Manhattan and went on to his training as an Air Force pilot in New Jersey. (I used to have a photo of him, a most gorgeous young man, standing beside the open cockpit of his small plane.) Some few months later, my mother called his supervisor, who summoned my father.

"I want to have this baby," she told him. "You have to marry me to give the child a name."

And so, his supervisor released him for a few hours, and he came in for a City Hall wedding. And then he went his way.

I remember seeing him once when he babysat for me when I was about three. There was one piece of pie, and I think he ate it. I have a postcard that says he sent me stuffed animals from FAO Schwartz.

The second time I saw him was when I was officially adopted by my new father (James Albert Mathieu), who I call my second father, for the purpose of clarity in this story. At seven years old, I stood between my first and second father before a judge's desk, my nose just reaching the desktop. I had some vague idea I was being given from one man I did not know to another man I had recently met. The judge, who looked important, signed some paper, and his clerk leaned over and blotted it. I then decided I wanted to be a judge and important and have someone to blot my signature.

And then my first father, or my biological father, whose name was Jimmy DeVries, disappeared from my life for about sixteen years.

Meanwhile, my second father (also a Jimmy) became the father I knew. He made me the best snowman. We watched television together. He helped my mother sew a Peter Pan costume for me when I wrote my now-forgotten dramatic sequel to that story, which was performed by my sixth-grade class. And then the marriage crumbled. My mother behaved so horribly that he seized her hand and broke her finger. They quarreled and hurled my toys around while I screamed, "Stop it, stop it!" He sat on the windowsill with one leg out the seventh-floor window, threatening to jump. I ran across the room, begging him not to do it.

He took his shoes from the closet and his shaving brush from the bathroom. He moved to a small apartment and eventually to Europe, and I didn't see him for a long time. The story was longer than this, of course, much more complex, but trying to fit all three fathers into one short essay is a job.

IN SEVENTH GRADE, I became intense and lifelong friends with a girl called Renée. Her parents had fled the Nazis after writing articles against them; her father, Henry, was Jewish and her mother was the socialist daughter of missionaries.

Renée took me home, and soon I was spending every weekend at their capacious apartment on the Upper West Side, whose long hallway was lined with books, several of which Henry had written. When I came to visit, Henry would say, "Ach, so!" with a wide smile, hurrying from his office where he had been writing some political article on his heavy black typewriter, which I inherited and kept for many years. He was a dear, benevolent man, and I adored him. His wife was a kind of saint.

Along with fifteen or more German escapees, Renée's family had shares in an old house in Sloatsburg, New York, with a brook on the property and a huge, enclosed porch. On the weekends in nice weather, Renée and I, and sometimes other friends, slept in a sort of dormitory that had been built next to the house for overflowing guests and noisy teenagers.

AGAIN, I COULD write chapters about this man who provided the emotional constancy in my life. It was an awful time with my mother's instability, and my second father across the ocean in Switzerland, where he was working and living with his new Swiss wife. My first father may have been in England; he lived there for a time.

I was living with my fiancé when my mother said one day, "I hear your father's back in town."

"Which father?" I asked.

"Your biological father," she said. "Your first father. He owns an antique shop in the East 60s."

I went to the shop, but he was out of town. I left my number. Then he called me back and my fiancé and I went to visit him, but my biological father was not alone. He had married a very unpleasant, older woman who was inexplicably nasty to me. The next day, he called me, rather ashamed, and said his wife was afraid I had come after him for her money and he couldn't see me. I never thought of money and was astonished.

A few years later, in my early twenties, my second father and his darling, sweet wife were living in Nuremberg and sent for me. They showed me Switzerland, parts of Germany, Austria, Paris, and the Loire Valley; and that is a complete story itself, four or five weeks of perfect heaven. Somewhere I have a picture of me before Mozart's birthplace in Salzburg. I came home to New York, married, and had children. When I had some money, in my later thirties, I began to visit my second father in Italian Switzerland and had the most extraordinary adventures. All of it shines in my life.

I RAISED MY sons and divorced. Through all of this, my third father, Henry, was the grandparent to my sons. (My mother didn't care much for children, so they hardly knew her.) One day when I was home, the phone rang, and it was my friend Renée. I can still hear her exact tone as if I memorized it forever. Her father had died of a heart attack. I said, "Oh," and other inconsequential things and went back to my work. I just tucked it away. Fourteen years later it came up in therapy, and I walked for an hour through Riverside Park sobbing as if it had no end.

Then when I was fifty, and my first book was in production, my younger son, Jesse, who was nineteen and home, called me at my office saying, "Ma, ma! Your father called!" And I said, "He called from Switzerland?" for we generally wrote. And my son said, "No, the other father."

"Which other father?" I asked and slowly, by process of elimination, it became clear to me. My biological father had called.

I called him back and his voice was so excited he stammered. It seems he had been in therapy also and discovered that his one great grief was that he had not been close to his father, and now he had a daughter he didn't know and wanted to meet me. So, I took the bus east and met him at the Hotel Wales where he was staying. He was having a bad time with his lover, the art historian John Richardson, but now he had found me.

I had an ecstatic time getting to know him. He was my treasure. But my second father (the other Jimmy), was not happy about this new relationship. "DeVries told me when he gave you up for adoption that he would never try to see you!" he said over the phone, this time long distance. So, I kept very quiet about it. I felt like an adulterous daughter.

I got to know much of myself by getting to know my biological father; we were so alike. I told him about my lover, and he told me about his lover. He took me to England, where we stayed in an apartment off the King's Road in Chelsea and went to Bath. But a few months after I returned, he got very upset with me. He had found out I didn't like Matisse and said seriously, irately, "Then you can't be my daughter!" He spoke badly to me, and I would have none of it.

Six months later, my biological father called from England to meet and start again. But his lover had left him, and he started to drink. He killed himself with an overdose of pills. Three days passed. His lawyers asked me to sign a paper stating that I would not contest his will, which he had changed after he quarreled with me. I had been his heir, which he changed to four old friends. I did not contest. I felt I couldn't while having another father (the second Jimmy) waiting for me in Italian Switzerland.

I wrote my first father a daughterly love letter, which was placed with his body when cremated. Again, I could write a lot about this complex man.

I CONTINUED TO go to Switzerland. My second father and stepmother had moved from a sixteenth-century house in a village to a larger town called Locarno on Lago Maggiore. I had married again to Russell, and we went together. How astonished Russell was at Europe and how he loved my father! (For by this time, James Albert Mathieu was my only father.)

My parents lived in a small housing complex on the side of a mountain, and you could walk to town in ten minutes or take the red funicular. We continued to visit every other year or so and sit on their terrace overlooking the foothills to the Alps and the lake and hear the bells ring from the pilgrimage church of Madonna del Sasso on the mountain. When we'd arrive, my father would call out to his wife, "The children are here!" which astonished my very grown husband.

My father trusted my husband; both were truly spiritual men. And one day in his eighties, he confided to Russell, "My life force is leaving me." We had gone to an ancient village and coming back, I saw my father concentrate on the drive with every ounce in him. He took us to the train to Zurich and stood waving on the platform.

A year or so later, the phone rang. (I have tears in my eyes writing it.) It was only eight in the morning, so I was surprised to hear my stepmother's voice, for she never called then. I asked, "Is everything all right?" and she said, "No, it isn't. Your father died."

To this day I look at the silent phone and will it to ring and hear his voice again, "Daughter, it's your father." I made an altar with candles, prayer beads, and a bottle of Ganges water (my parents followed Hinduism), and his photos. I sat before it many times.

So, there it is, three fathers. I consider myself very fortunate. I hear their voices together calling my name, hurrying from rooms to welcome me. What gift can I give them? I loved them dearly all the time when I had them in my life. That is all we can give to each other in the end and the best thing.

I MAK SICCAR (I MAKE SURE)

by Katherine Kirkpatrick

IT'S A JOYFUL scene and all I can do is smile. The cousins brandish plastic swords and daggers as they chase after each other, screaming, on the wide green lawn of a midwestern state park during our Kirkpatrick family reunion. Some don tartan sashes and velveteen cloaks and wear tartan kilts over their shorts. One carries a round shield taped with a printed paper image of our family crest. A trio of girls in sashes stand in a circle and blast out squeaky noises on plastic recorders while a three-year-old boy in a purple cape and Burger King crown beats a toy drum.

My vantage point at the top of the hill near the inn gives me a good view of the costumed kids, the lawn edging into a wide blue lake. My vantage point as a middle-aged adult who has been attending these reunions my whole life gives me another kind of perspective. The extended family, all descendants of midwestern pioneers Austin and Sarah Kirkpatrick, who married in 1864, meet for one weekend at a midwestern state park every three years (though this time because of COVID it has been four years). With every reunion, my love for these relatives grows stronger and our bonds deepen. Many knew my parents and my grandparents, and the eldest of them knew my great-grandparents. My generation has seen each other and our children grow up; and those junior swordsmen and swashbucklers, as well as the toddlers crawling in and out of the conical castle play tent (adorned with a dragon and jousting knights), are my age group's grandchildren.

The inn's dining room opens for lunch, and I join my sister, Jen, and brother-in-law, Eric, in retrieving and packing up the costumes for tonight's cookout. The Scotland-themed festivities, organized by Jen, will feature a parade, children's play, games, and a group photo. Jen informs me, with a roll of the eyes, that she's received two comments from concerned parents about the arsenal of toy weaponry available. I laugh. Well, at least there are no toy guns, and I've noticed that the kids are being careful not to hurt each other. They're good kids and they're clearly having a good time. What's important to me is that everyone, young and old, liberals and conservatives, comes together as a family. Jen and Eric, and their carload of outfits and props, which they've transported eight-and-a-half hours, halfway across the country from their home on the East Coast, greatly add to our group experience. I've come from Seattle, and the play I've scripted and family trivia I've collected are my contributions.

AS A MOTHER of gender non-conforming twins, one of whom has moved ahead with a legal name and gender change, I'm particularly sensitive to criticism from conservatives. I have found only love and acceptance at family reunions. My cousins who live in the red states are among the friendliest people on earth. But unfortunately, I'm always a little on edge in case someone should make a remark. For two days during the last reunion, both twins, perceiving that the other teens did not like them, holed themselves up in their room at the inn. Finally, they joined the pack in running around on the big lawn in an evening capture-the-flag game. They wanted to come to this reunion, but stayed behind because of their jobs as camp counselors.

I think of them now as I ride on the lake in a pontoon boat, crowded with a bunch of distant midwestern cousins who are mostly younger than me. I take the opportunity to gather tidbits for this evening's trivia game by questioning some cousins I hardly know about their jobs, hobbies, and families. In every case, I'm reminded of how devoted my relatives are to their families, their churches, and their communities. I like and admire them.

And yet, stray thoughts pertaining to no one here crop up in my mind. An attractive young couple has just moved from one red state to an even more conservative one, where medical gender-transition treatments and surgeries are outlawed for minors. If I'd lived in their state, I could have been arrested for child abuse by letting my son make his own bodily choices. There's a side of me that wants to lecture anyone willing to listen about the high suicide rates among transgender people and the vital importance of putting laws in place that afford them freedom and protection.

Wait! Stop! I tell myself. *Why worry about this now?* My children and I live in a blue state. What's more, I doubt these young people agree with their state laws. Or even if they do, why should that stop us from being friends? It's a beautiful sunny day on the lake, and I'm not at the reunion to change anyone's mind about LGBTQ rights, abortion rights, climate change, Mexican immigrants and the border, or anything else.

There's a phrase I like: "There by the grace of God go I." I can easily trace why I grew up in a blue state on the East Coast as opposed to the Midwest. Five generations ago, my great-great grandparents Austin and Sarah, midwestern corn farmers, had seven children who lived to adulthood. One of these, my great-grandfather Fred, moved off the family farm to open up a dry goods store adjoining a newly established university in a nearby town. Fred's four brothers, including Ora, remained farmers in the Midwest. Fred's son, my grandfather Sidney Dale, attended the university, became a chemical engineer and magazine publisher, and eventually moved to the East Coast for his work. By and large, the "Freds" at our reunion have grown up in blue states on the East and West Coasts while the "Oras," who greatly multiplied and represent the majority of the people here, mainly stayed in the middle of the country. Things are changing, though. The members of my children's generation—fifth generation Austins and Sarahs—live all over, many in cities; and though there are still Ora corn farmers in the family, they are few.

My branch of the Kirkpatrick family immigrated to America from Scotland in the 1700s. That rather distant connection to the mother country nevertheless still looms large in the imagination. Hence, at least half the group at the family cookout wears reunion T-shirts featuring the family coat of arms with its bloody dagger on top. The hooded blanket of our dark green Colquhoun tartan serves well as a banner; I hang it over a fence near the picnic shelter. Out come the weaponry, cloaks, kilts, sashes, and two toy castles, representing London, England, and Dumfries, Scotland, in the year 1306 for a theater-in-the-round, picnic-shelter production of *I Mak Siccar: An Adventure from History*.

The majority of the kids miss the rehearsal for the play because they are swimming or boating, so those who show up have their choice of parts. A petite five-year-old girl named Anna, who has remarkable lung capacity, plays Sir Roger Kirkpatrick, our illustrious (or infamous) ancestor. I enlist one of my good-natured, thirty-something second cousins to portray the famed Scottish warrior Robert the Bruce, another major role. He wears sunglasses, a long shirt, a kilt over his shorts, a plastic dagger tucked into his belt, and sneakers. Kids who show up after the rehearsal are added to the chase scene, in which a juvenile

King Edward of England and his entourage race after Robert the Bruce, circumventing the picnic area.

Robert the Bruce stabs his competitor for the crown, John Comyn, also known as the Red Comyn, in the chapel. Bruce rushes out of the chapel and says to one of his attendants, "I must be off. I've tried to slay the Red Comyn, but I don't think I've done it. He may come after me."

"You have a doubt?" said his buddy, Roger Kirkpatrick. "*I mak siccar!*" That's Scots Gaelic for "I make sure."

Once assured by her mother that it's okay to use her "outside voice," little Anna holds her sword up in the air and belts out "*I mak siccar*" as loudly and enthusiastically as any adult could have done. She's a real crowd pleaser.

Roger Kirkpatrick enters the chapel to ensure that Comyn is dead. He isn't, so Roger finishes him off. Robert the Bruce becomes King of Scotland (with a Burger King crown). Next, King Robert bestows on his partner in crime the title of "Sir" Roger and grants him his own coat of arms. You guessed it. The armorial, flanked by lions, presents Roger's bloody dagger on its crest and bears the family motto "*I mak siccar.*"

Prompted by the audience, Anna does an encore of her famous line. And in an unscripted bonus, a groundhog discovers a piece of fried chicken on the grass and stands on its back legs eating it just a short distance away from the picnic shelter. Photo opportunities abound.

After dinner, the fanfare continues with a costumed parade. Jen takes out the large, magnificent banners she has made with gold coats of arms against backgrounds of red and royal blue. The coats of arms not only represent the Colquhoun clan (which includes the Kirkpatricks) but the coats of arms of other families here who married Kirkpatricks. The reunion keeps getting better with the arrival of a Highland bagpiper. Never mind that he's unable to walk without a walker. His haunting and explosive notes drown out the conversations and the kids' shrill-sounding recorders. Delightedly, I snap pictures on my cell phone as my sister and the kids, waving their banners, parade around the picnic area and around the bagpiper who is puffing out "Scotland the Brave."

Long after the parade ends and the bagpiper departs, the children continue to run about the lawn in their capes and tartan sashes. Some with plastic daggers and swords chase after my brother-in-law, Eric, who plays the part of a slain warrior falling dead on the grass. We're certainly getting a lot of mileage out of our Scottish heritage theme, especially the one gory incident that happened in Dumfries in 1306. The family trivia contest, our next activity, includes both family history and brag-worthy news of present-day family—such as, who among us is an expert in cryptocurrency, and who climbed Mount Kilimanjaro since the last reunion?

The following day, our group meets together one last time at an outdoor church service. The minister, one of several in the family, announces recent births, marriages, and deaths. At the service's conclusion, one of my distant cousins sings the "*I Mak Siccar*" ballad he'd written. Maybe one day someone will come up with another anecdote from history highlighting a Kirkpatrick ancestor. For now, this rather dubious claim to fame on the part of Roger Kirkpatrick serves as a unifier, or at least as a colorful backdrop. Of course, it's family connection of the last few generations that primarily bonds us.

It is hard for me to say goodbye to everyone; the three-years wait in between reunions feels like a long time. What tugs at my heart the most is to hug my older relations, several who are ninety or nearly ninety. I may never see them again.

RETURNING HOME TURNS out to be more of an adjustment than I'd anticipated, and not just because of the changes in time (two hours earlier), and in temperature (very hot to cool), and landscape (open and flat to forested and mountainous). At home, I am among fellow liberals who are reading the news and talking almost incessantly about conservative lawmakers ruining our country. And I had just spent four days in a red state surrounded by conservative relatives who never once brought up significant issues.

Did I let my trans children and trans friends down? No, I think not. By referring to my children as their chosen pronouns this past weekend, I'd made our situation evident. If anyone had wanted to talk to me about them or my views, I certainly would have—at length. And if I'd asked my relatives to express their views on political or religious subjects, they would have—at length. One of these days, a relative may be in the position of raising a transgender child and seek me out, and I would volunteer my help.

Now, I appreciate the generosity and kindness of my relatives. I appreciate them for being the genuinely good people they are. Love flows between people when we do not judge each other. Our family reunion affirmed this truth to me. We are all connected. I have no doubt. *I mak siccar.*

Katherine and bagpiper.

King Edward and the players perform.

Prompt: Write about a place that is important to you . . . where do you long to return?

GHOSTS OF CHANOINESSE

by Rhonda Hunt-Del Bene

Paris, France
October 2012

IN THE MIDDLE of Paris, the River Seine parts, and its water diverts around two islands. The smaller island, Île Saint-Louis, is primarily composed of upscale residential buildings and boutiques. On the larger island, Île de la Cité, are various structures. There is a large hospital named Hôtel-Dieu—Hotel of God. Each time I walk past it, I am reminded of the song "Hotel California" by the American rock band, the Eagles, in which the singer tells us there is never a problem checking in, the issue is checking out. I assume he means via the morgue.

The Conciergerie is also here. It is the prison where Marie Antoinette awaited her turn at the guillotine in 1793. However, the most famous structure on the island is the thirteenth-century French Gothic cathedral, Notre-Dame de Paris—Our Lady of Paris.

Île de la Cité is my *hood,* as this is where my favorite Parisian apartment is located, just steps from Notre-Dame. Walking home one night, I made a slight detour to the cathedral, which I preferred to visit after the circus wagons full of tourists departed for the day. That evening, I wanted to place my hands on the ancient façade to see if I received any visions of ghosts trapped inside. No ghosts appeared, but I could still feel the warmth of the autumn day lingering on the stones, even though the surrounding air turned chilly.

I stepped back from the building to look for the statue of Saint-Denis. He is my favorite among the sainted figures adorning the front of the cathedral because he is headless and stands holding his severed head in his hands. Nowadays, he is the Patron Saint of Paris, but back in the third century, when Christians were pariahs, Saint-Denis was a missionary from Italy who was so successful in converting the people of France to Christianity that he was beheaded. It seems the French have long been fond of separating people from their heads. According to legend, Saint-Denis picked up his severed head and walked to Montmartre.

As I left the headless Saint-Denis and started toward my apartment on Rue Chanoinesse, the words of Rudyard Kipling played in my own intact head: "If you can keep your head when all about you / Are losing theirs and blaming it on you," but my thoughts were interrupted by a black cat. Just as I reached the edge of the cathedral's north tower, the cat jumped from behind the hedges and onto a short cement wall anchoring the wrought-iron fence that encircled the edifice. I stopped to greet him. We had a brief exchange; I spoke to him in French, and he responded in an assortment of meows. I started back on my way, but he stayed by my side, walking on the cement base of the fence, and making a serpentine pattern in and out of the iron rods, meowing as he meandered.

TYPICALLY, I WOULD have thought a black cat was an omen of bad luck except for an incident that happened a couple of weeks earlier, in Rome, when my Latvian friend Marko was taking me back to my hotel on his *motorino*. It was late and to save time, Marko was driving the wrong way on a one-way street, creeping along slowly, with the headlight off, in case the *polizia* appeared from a side street. Suddenly, a black cat darted in front of us. I leaned forward, speaking to the back of Marko's helmeted head, and told him that in America, a black cat crossing one's path is a bad omen. He turned his head slightly toward me and said that in Latvia, it was a sign of good luck. As if on cue, a *polizia* cruiser pulled from a side street and headed toward us, its headlights shining on us like an accusatory interrogation lamp. Marko quickly pulled into a parking space and hit the kill switch, shutting off the motor. After the cruiser passed, we exploded into side-splitting laughter, thinking about the portent of the black cat. After composing ourselves, Marko turned the switch to "run," revved the motor, and backed into the street. We continued as we had before, traveling in the wrong direction.

THE NOTRE-DAME CAT continued to walk with me, deftly threading his way through the wrought iron, as if this is how he always walked along this fence. I thought of the Roman cat and how we overlay our own interpretation of what is good and bad upon the events in our lives.

The fence ended at the bridge to Île Saint-Louis. The cat gave a final salutation in meows, jumped into the hedges behind the cathedral, and disappeared into the black night.

Arriving at the apartment, I entered the code to open the *portail* and stepped into the courtyard. A fine rain began to fall, making it even spookier to walk past the engraved marble-slab grave markers near the building entrance. *Why did they bury people in the courtyard?* The spiral staircase was dimly lighted, and I had to balance myself against the wall to climb the wedge-shaped wooden stairs that were barely wide enough for a size 5 shoe.

Once inside the apartment, I opened the windows to the autumnal night sky. The long days of summer had departed, and ghostly clouds skimmed the spire of Notre-Dame, visible from the open window. The moon moved lazily in and out of the India-ink clouds, seemingly circling the spire, and together they created an ethereal dance, twirling slowly as if they were trinkets on a baby's mobile suspended over a crib, set in motion by a breath of wind.

EARLIER IN THE day, I had gone to Père Lachaise Cemetery to lay a rose on the grave of Jim Morrison, of the famous rock band, The Doors. Morrison had died in Paris in 1971. As I watched the night sky, I played his song, "Riders on the Storm." With its ominous rattling of thunder, and the lonely piano notes mimicking the sound of falling rain, the music created an otherworldly accompaniment to the haunting moon dance . . . and my thoughts turned to the other occupant of this apartment at 16 Rue Chanoinesse—the ghost.

THE CHANOINESSE APARTMENT was a lovely place. Built in the 1700s, it has retained its old-world charm as the wood ceiling beams and terracotta floor tiles are original. Because the floor was uneven, one must be attentive when traversing it. Glenn, my landlord, decorated the apartment with an eclectic array of antiques and second-hand furniture from varying time periods and styles, mostly purchased at *Le Marché aux Puces* (Paris's famous flea market). At the heart of the living room was a fireplace with scroll-leaf pilasters and a dramatic, black marble mantel. Even though I was not a morning person, I didn't mind the pealing of the bells that began every morning at 7:00 a.m. I found the sound to be meditative as I imagined the saints and sinners making their way to mass and pondering what sins they might divulge later in confession.

I felt at home here, even though the place was haunted.

My husband and I both had experiences with *him*, the ghost, on separate occasions, while staying at the apartment alone. We each had *dreamed* that someone was poking us in the back. And when we awakened, we were lying sideways along the end of the bed. Our Chanoinesse neighbor told us that, according to legend, the first occupant of the apartment was a priest from Notre-Dame, who was supposedly one of the two buried in the courtyard. So, I assumed the ghost must be the long-dead priest. However, a man who claimed to be a spiritual medium told me otherwise.

While dining at a restaurant on the Champs-Élysées, I met a couple from Atlanta. The man said he was a medium; and since they were staying on the adjacent island, Île-Saint-Louis, I invited them over to see what he *sensed*. "I'm not getting an *ecclesiastical* energy," he said. "Instead, I perceive it to be the spirit of a businessman who lived here at one time. He is very curious about you because you are a businesswoman who would have been an anomaly in his time."

After the medium left, I poured a glass of Haut-Médoc wine and opened the windows to gaze at Notre-Dame while I thought about what he had just said. Little did I know it would be the last time I would see its magnificent spire.

I LONG TO return to the apartment on Rue Chanoinesse, but alas, all that remains are my memories of life there . . . memories that visit me from time to time, like the ghost. The Notre-Dame spire is no longer there. It was the first architectural element to fall during the violent fire of 2019.

In 2016, Glenn sold the apartment to someone who inhabits it full time. I wonder if the ghost haunts the new occupant.

16 Rue Chanoinesse.

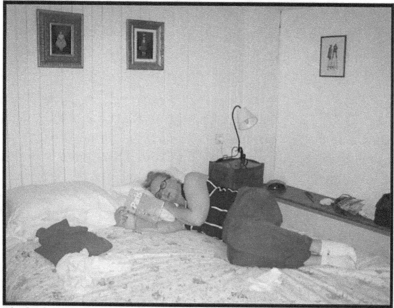

The bedroom where the ghost visits. Rhonda in bed reading about Paris.

MY UNCLE JOHNNY

by Stephanie Cowell

WHEN I WAS a little girl, I adored my uncle Johnny. I still do, years after his too-early death. There was, however, no more unlikely pair than he and I. He knew nothing about children except that they were small and their minds worked in odd ways.

My uncle Johnny was my mother's eldest brother. I can't remember when I first knew him, but he must have hovered uneasily over my cradle, peering down. I tottered to him sometime later, because I remember his thick fingers in a hand open to me, extended. At an early age, I sensed his uneasiness.

My uncle lived in an elegant residency hotel in Midtown Manhattan, then moderately priced, which is why he took it, since he had no use for elegance. I knew he loved scotch and water, swirling gently around fat ice cubes in the glass. The ice clinked when he raised the glass. I think he was a moderate drinker, but moderate in the late 1940s and early fifties could be considered excessive today. I knew he played bridge, and had seen a picture of him, hunched, his rumpled white shirt over his round belly, at a card table. For relaxation, he enjoyed excursions on sport-fishing boats. Occasionally, I received a postcard from his fishing trips, but all they said was, "Love, Uncle John." Somewhere, there was a picture of him, shirtsleeves rolled up, leaning on the boat rail crowded by other laconic men, each with a fishing line dangling into the seawater.

Johnny was rather bald also, and I think did not like the sun, but I've seen photos of him at the beach with my mother and the very tiny girl that was myself. Near the water, Uncle Johnny wore a hat, his shirtsleeves rolled, his trousers rolled to his knee. And always, a fat cigar was in his hand.

MY MOTHER WAS frequently appalled. "I am appalled!" was her favorite phrase. She was mostly appalled (Not always; everyone has personality contradictions.) by anything that was not fashionable or in great taste. (I had terrible taste in her mind.) She worked as an haute couture fashion artist for *Vogue*; and since he was fourteen years old, Uncle Johnny worked at General Electric. He became a salesman of carpet cleaners. As the oldest sibling, Uncle Johnny was the man of the house, the breadwinner at whatever small wages he earned. He was a company man before he had to shave.

Once, we went to see my uncle demonstrate his carpet cleaner in a hardware store. At least twenty people were there. He puffed his cigar between phrases. I was enchanted. He was a star.

"He's had a hard life," my mother would say. "Going to work at such a young age. General Electric used him up, treated him badly. A salesman! But . . . poor man."

And my little mind would try to imagine the thin, not very tall, boy of fourteen, living in some shabby dwelling in Schenectady (the cradle of GE) with his widowed mom and brothers and sisters. One brother became a construction worker and the other a bookie. (I figured that it had something to do with horse racing and was illegal.) My fat aunt Gertie (of whom I wrote a story published in *Seventeen* magazine long ago) suspected everything in the world that did not come through the static of our wood radio. The youngest was my dark-eyed, seething, brilliant mother.

So, there I was, his little shy niece. And he would come visit us and not say much; but I felt his solidity, which was a blessing to me with such a mercurial mother. He was an example of dull and ordinary to her, yet I loved him. Not that he knew how to make conversation with me . . . with anyone. He spoke a word or two.

He must have taken me out several times, as uncles do, but I clearly remember only twice. When I was about seven years old, he took me to dinner in the dining room of his Shoreham Hotel. I wore my prettiest dress and was thrilled to take his hand. We probably went by taxi. In the enormous dining room, we sat at a table with a white tablecloth so thick it could be turned into a serviceable winter quilt. And he leaned his head down. He may have been a little deaf by then to talk to me . . . about what I don't know. But I was too sidetracked to hear him because in my pocket I had the fifty cents my mother gave me to buy his favorite cigar. It was a fifty-cent cigar, then the very best. That sum of money had bought many popsicles.

At any rate, I followed my mother's plan, excused myself to use the ladies' room, but diverted to the hotel newsstand, fingering the money in my pocket. I stood before the huge display of newspapers and candy and cigars, pointing to the one I wanted. (That a seven-year-old girl could buy a cigar is something from the far past of New York City, but I think the counterman trusted my tale that it was for my uncle.)

I recrossed the dining room and climbed into my chair. I hid the cigar, somehow. As I was waiting to give it to Uncle Johnny after dinner, he took another of the *very same expensive cigars* from his pocket and casually lit it. (Cigars in dining rooms are also long gone.) I felt a little crushed; I felt redundant. I inched the one I had purchased humbly across the thick white tablecloth to him. I think he thanked me. The intricacies of such a situation were beyond his limited vocabulary. He muttered; he looked grave.

Would anything I gave anyone be enough? I wondered. Still, I think he was touched.

MY UNCLE JOHNNY bought me gifts each year. He had not much imagination when it came to gift giving (neither do I most of the time), so for birthdays and holidays, he bought me soft leather moccasins and Brownie box cameras. He bought the moccasins in larger sizes so I could grow into them. The cameras were the same model. For many years, in one of our closets on the upper shelf, sat several cameras and several pairs of moccasins.

But he also gave me, totally unwittingly, two gifts that changed the course of my life.

The first involved my strong memory of an outing, to see the musical *Peter Pan* on Broadway, starring Mary Martin. I was ten or eleven years old. He bought seats for the first row, center mezzanine, and I was fascinated. I had been to several Broadway dramas and musicals by this time, but this was beyond magical. When I talked about it at intermission, I babbled something about "when Peter threw the fairy dust."

"It's not really fairy dust, it's glitter," said my uncle. I muttered something . . . but to me it *was* fairy dust; it *was* real. I felt sad; my uncle couldn't see the genuine thing when it was there.

But the experience did change my life because I then decided to become a writer and go on the stage. In sixth grade, I wrote a sequel to *Peter Pan*, which my teacher thought was remarkable for a child of my age and produced it. I was Peter. My life in the arts was affirmed and confirmed. I acted, I sang, I wrote. That was how to express my shy inner self. That was my world. Many years later, it still is.

Then came Johnny's second life-changing gift, a heavy book called *Milton Cross' Complete Stories of the Great Operas*. Why he should give me such a thing, I don't know. I had never heard opera; no one in my family knew anything about it; and certainly, Johnny was ignorant. Opera became my life for many years.

THEN JOHNNY WAS retiring. My mom speculated that he was redundant. "They made him go," she said indignantly. "After all these years, those worthless pieces of shit! He gave his life to them."

Being in my teens and knowing nothing of such things, I only felt the sadness. I went to the retirement party and stood behind tall people (I have spent my life standing behind tall people), and he made a speech, probably very brief. People spoke about him. Everyone clapped. Everyone drank. He got some gifts. But he seemed lost. He had been a GE man all his life and now was no longer one.

Johnny was a bachelor until his fifties or sixties and then married a big, hearty woman called Olive with a big, hearty laugh. My mother was, yes, "appalled" by her—and that he had married at all. Perhaps she expected her brother John to always linger at the edge of our lives, in case we needed him.

"Well, it's time he had a life of his own," my mother relented at first, but she was, of course, appalled that John and Olive had love or God forbid sex. Eventually, my mother so insulted Olive that from then on, I went alone to visit him. I was in my early twenties then and living in scrappy conditions in the Bronx with the man I would marry. My uncle muttered behind his cigar; it did not seem right for me to live in a neighborhood he didn't consider safe or decent.

THE UNTHINKABLE HAPPENED and my world shifted. Johnny and Olive moved to Florida. She may have still been working and transferred her job. The Shoreham Hotel was empty of them. She wrote to me maybe once a year. Then came terrible news by letter from Olive. My uncle Johnny had died of a heart attack from his diabetes. I was shocked. My mother said he never should have married that woman who was as "ordinary as dirt." Now and then I think she also said, "Maybe she made him happy. He didn't have an easy life."

In a mental list of things that I regret in my life, I did not answer Olive's letter. I couldn't acknowledge my uncle's death, or maybe it was just part of his leaving my life. I resented that he was gone, or my own life was going too fast. And I was a young mom, singing my first roles in opera, and trying to make a few dollars sewing.

Dear Uncle Johnny! I wish I could have the address to send this little memory piece to you now. People stray into our lives and become so seminal; they change everything with a smile, a look, a puff of smoke, a row of too-large moccasins that I had to grow into year by year. I don't know who used the last of them. Perhaps my mother gave them to Goodwill.

Stephanie and Uncle Johnny, December 1945.

A BIBLICAL KING...
AND ITALIAN ICONS

by Rhonda Hunt-Del Bene

Firenze, Italia
Novembre 2019

I SIT IN my political science class and watch the rain, tuning out Dr. Caputi's lecture while an errant mosquito makes its way toward me through an open window.

"Why don't the Italians believe in putting screens on windows?" I think.

"And why, even in the cold and rain of November, are *le zanzare* (mosquitos) still ubiquitous and merciless, seeking out my *sangue dolce* (sweet blood) and torturing me?"

My attention turns back to Dr. Caputi only when I hear her assign us to go into the streets and find an object that represents the philosophy of Karl Marx in his *Communist Manifesto*, quoting the line, "All that is solid melts into air, all that is holy is profaned."

"In essence, nothing retains its original sanctity," she emphasizes.

I step out into the rain and walk to the Basilica di Santa Croce (*Holy Cross)*, since it is close to the university and Dr. Caputi used it as an example in her lecture. I stop to pay homage to the statue of Dante Alighieri that stands by the steps. This Dante is my touchstone. My apartment is just around the corner and every day I pass by and thank him for the beautiful language that, through his literature, became the basis of the Italian we speak today. If I could have reached the hem of Dante's cloak, I would have touched it, like the woman in the Bible who touched the hem of Jesus's robe, seeking to find some mystical powers it might impart.

I turn to look at the steps of the Basilica since Dr. Caputi specifically highlighted them as exemplifying Marx's theory. She told us that Santa Croce, also called the Temple of Italian Glories, was built to house the remains of some of Italy's most exalted—Michelangelo, Galileo, Machiavelli.

"Now," she said, "the steps of this once hallowed church are used as a meeting place for drunken debauchery."

I continue to Via dei Neri, cursing the rain and dodging the umbrellas of wayward pedestrians with heads down and feet plowing forward, when I discover a little shop named *Trottola,* which means a "spinning top" in Italian. In the window are displayed Pop Art souvenirs depicting Michelangelo's David as Superman and Ronald McDonald—an ironic modern twist on traditional fine art values. There is also an assortment of neon-colored miniature Davids with price tags strung around their necks like nooses.

"Surely I can find something here that will epitomize Marx's theory," I think as I push open the door.

Inside *Trottola,* I find even more portrayals of David. Michelangelo's masterpiece is one of the most recognizable pieces of art in the world; and in Italy, the statue is simply referred to as *Il David.* As I browse the merchandise, I am reminded of its history.

In 1499, Michelangelo was only twenty-four and had just completed the *Pietà* for St. Peter's Basilica in Rome. His hauntingly beautiful statue depicts the suffering of the Madonna as she holds the lifeless body of her son, Jesus Christ, following his deposition from the cross. The young sculptor's work was so widely praised and admired that the Vatican immediately commissioned him to create a biblical David in Firenze (Florence) for the Cattedrale di Santa Maria del Fiore (*il Duomo*).

When David was finished, the Vatican deemed him too magnificent to be placed high up on the cathedral, where he could not be sufficiently appreciated. For nearly four hundred years, *Il David* stood in the Piazza della Signoria. But time, weather, and pigeons damaged his beauty, so he was moved to the Galleria dell'Accademia, which is where I saw him for the first time when I was nineteen years old.

NEAR THE CASH register at *Trottola,* I find a book bag imprinted with the torso of *Il David* covered in tattoos.

"A 'Tatted-Up'[10] David!" I think to myself. "This is perfect!"

As I contemplate buying the bag, Alessandro, the shop's owner, explains the significance of this David's body art. It includes some of the most iconic Florentine figures: Botticelli's *Venus* is conspicuously displayed on his abs; *il Duomo*—his original destination that was never reached—is emblazoned on his right thigh; and Michelangelo, David's own "God and Creator," appears on his right shoulder. On his neck is written a "3" and "1501-1504," indicating the number of years it took to create him and the years in which he was created. On his right wrist, he boasts that he generates "Eight Million Euros" a year through tourism. On his left forearm, he declares that he is "*un re biblica*," a biblical king.

Alessandro deciphers the *tatuaggi* (tattoos) for me, and I try to remember exactly how I felt the first time I saw *Il David* at the Accademia. I recall walking down the long hall to the gallery where he stood. He was visible during the entire approach to the room, and he was *mozzafiato* (breathtaking). The tour guide explained how innovative it was that Michelangelo depicted David in this pose. Other Florentine artists, such as Verrocchio, Ghiberti, and Donatello, portrayed him after his victory, standing triumphantly over the slain Goliath. Michelangelo, instead, captured him at the apex of his concentration prior to battle. He stood relaxed, resting in a classical pose known as *contrapposto*, but his eyes were intense and contemplative.

Alessandro reminds me that David was once the mighty biblical king of the ancient United Kingdom of Israel. This is not a fact I attach to *Il David* when I saw him.

"But King David was a flawed man who fell from the grace of the Lord because of his lust for Bathsheba," Alessandro continues.

". . . *All that is holy is profaned.*" The words directed by Dr. Caputi come back to me.

I purchase the book bag and an assortment of oversized postcards of *Il David* as Superman and Ronald McDonald, feeling a bit guilty for buying them. As I step back onto the *strada,* my thoughts are as gloomy as the downpour, reflecting sadness for a once-hallowed king and his mighty fall. I think how the "aura" of a great piece of art can diminish through the perspective of distance and time, and how a lauded art object can descend into Pop Art. I wonder what Michelangelo would think of this modern treatment of *Il David*. Would he find these images profane? Even

---

10 Urban Slang Dictionary. Tatted-up: a person covered with tattoos.

he destroyed one of his sculptures with a hammer when he was dissatisfied with the result. Would he take a hammer to these "afterlife images" of his great masterpiece?

THAT EVENING I return to my apartment via my usual path, passing again Santa Croce, grateful that the rain has stopped. I pause to watch a noisy group assembling on the steps. The ringleader of the revelers, dressed in a black musketeer-style hat with a jaunty white plume and thigh-high Puss-in-Boots style *stivali,* waves his long cloak wildly back and forth, while brandishing a bottle of wine like a fencing sword.

"Che cosa state festeggiando?"[11] I yell up to him.

"Vivere (life)," he replies as he uncorks the bottle, takes a swig, and makes a gesture of *un brindisi* (a toast) toward me.

I laugh as I walk away, thinking, "If Karl Marx were here tonight, he would shake his head and say, '*Nothing retains its original sanctity.*'"

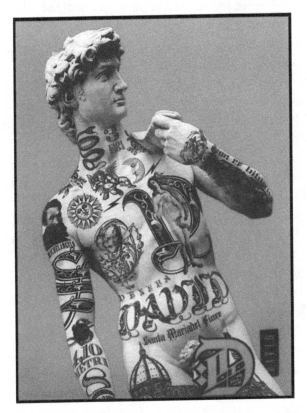

---

[11] In Italian: What are you celebrating?

DAD'S LAST BLESSING

by Katherine Kirkpatrick

I LEAPT OUT of bed when the phone rang at 3:00 a.m. Already I knew that the news couldn't be good.

I'd only been sleeping lightly in anticipation of an early alarm to catch the flight from Seattle to Long Island, New York, to attend my beloved older brother's second marriage ceremony. "Hello," I mumbled, not yet alert.

"It's Sid." His voice sounded low and strained. "Dad just passed away." I collapsed into the hallway chair.

Heart failure had taken our adored father, Dale Kirkpatrick, in his sleep. "What about your wedding?" I asked.

"Everyone's here. Instead of having the wedding tomorrow, we'll have Dad's memorial service." The hasty change of plans reminded me of Sid's resilience. "Nancy and I will get married the next day." He had found a gracious match in his fiancée.

At the beach cabana dinner, the night before, our "people person" father had delighted in the joyful gathering of extended family reunited for the wedding. No one had felt overly concerned about Dad's shortness of breath, since it had been typical of his ongoing heart trouble and lack of exercise. Perhaps I should have foreseen Dad's death; he was seventy-eight, overweight, a diabetic with high blood pressure, and had experienced multiple heart attacks and strokes.

He had suffered an almost unbelievable number of mishaps and accidents. While he trained as an aircraft gunner for the Navy in Pensacola, Florida in 1945 at the end of WWII, a tire on his A-26 bomber burst when landing. He miraculously survived the crash. Decades later, he broke his neck while teaching my brother to dive at the cabana beach. In the final years of his life, he swung himself stiffly into car seats because of his hip replacement surgeries. A perpetually swollen left foot from poor circulation meant that he lumbered along in an open-toed sandal, even in winter. Doctors discussed the possibility of amputating his foot. But he possessed such great vitality, and had up to this point cheerfully, even casually, survived every kind of medical challenge that it seemed inconceivable to me that he should ever die.

I listened numbly with the phone in my hand.

Sid said he loved me and would see me soon, leaving me in the swirling vortex of grief, memories, and worries about what the coming days would bring.

My husband was ready with a hug and a guiding hand through the darkness as we returned to bed for the remaining minutes before my alarm. As I prayed and cried in the stillness, my mind quickly listed the sorrows and blessings of the upcoming back-to-back funeral and wedding. I offered thanks that Sid and Nancy and their soon-to-be blended family of four teenagers had been staying in my parents' home, so Mom wasn't alone when she discovered that Dad had died. And how fortunate that Dad had departed this life in happy anticipation of his only son's wedding.

But he wouldn't see Sid and Nancy get married.

And if I'd traveled just one day earlier, I could have had that one last visit with Dad that Sid and our sister, Jen, had enjoyed. Well, it was what it was. I'd planned to keep my visit short because of my four-year-old twins at home.

PREPARATIONS FOR THE memorial were well underway by the time I arrived on Long Island that evening. My brother, and my sister, Jen, had decided that all three of us would give tributes. This came as another shock to me. I was terrified of public speaking and only had one night to come up with a script.

Since my parents' house was already full, I slept at the next-door neighbor's home of my high school French teacher, Irmgard Whitney, who had become a lifelong friend. There, I had space to pray, prepare my tribute, and steady myself amid my sadness and jet lag. She ironed my clothes and made herself available when I felt ready to talk. I took swims in her family's pool, and the very cold water invigorated me when my body felt rigid with tension.

Dad's memorial took place at my parents' church, the Setauket Presbyterian, on a sweltering day in the last weekend in June. As a proud Scotsman (never mind that our branch of the Kirkpatrick clan has lived in American since the 1700s), my father had cherished having a bagpiper for family weddings and funerals. Outside the centuries-old white, steepled edifice, the deep rumble of the bagpipes began. The piper boomed out "Scotland the Brave" and something in my heart burst open. The mournful sounds seeped into my bones, finally allowing me to weep. I not only wept for the loss of my father, but for the slow decline and disappearance of my mother, already some years into her dementia.

Despite the short notice, the church filled almost to capacity with the friends Dad had made through tennis, bridge, the cabana beach, Rotary, charity organizations, and his work as a travel agent. Everyone in the close-knit community knew him—his friendliness and his universal acceptance of people made him popular. Light poured through the church's large, plate-glass windows, and the aged building creaked and held the heat and humidity. All around me, people fanned themselves with their programs. I later learned that in the balcony near an open window, a bee stung my fifteen-year-old niece Alice and she had to be taken to the emergency room.

I took comfort in hearing Reverend Jim Wallace's Scottish brogue as he officiated, remembering my father's joyous enthusiasm for this minister. In the over five decades my parents had belonged to the church, they had seen a lot of clergymen come and go. Reverend Wallace's arrival, straight from Edinburgh, in Dad's last few years, made my father's life complete.

Struck by grief as I was, I didn't recall exactly what I or anyone else said in their tributes. Though the day remains a jumble to me now, my father's larger-than-life personality shone forth. He had assumed the fearless (some might say foolhardy) attitude that if there was something he wanted to do, he would just do it. After considerable success as a salesman of industrial metals for Edgecombe Steel, Dad passed up a well-paying offer to become a "company man" in higher management for a freer life on the move. An entrepreneur at heart, he started (and folded) several businesses, including one as a middleman for American enterprises and Caribbean metal-working shops, that to his great delight often took him to Puerto Rico.

His Navy experience gave him a lifelong interest in aviation. Dad originally wanted to become a commercial pilot. He never realized that dream, apparently because his eyesight wasn't good enough to meet regulations.

A man who always mixed work with pleasure, Dad opened a travel agency and developed a sideline of organizing trips with his tennis-playing friends. Dad brought the family to many destinations around the world, including his last big trip to Scotland with his children and grandchildren to celebrate my parents' fiftieth wedding anniversary and his seventy-fifth birthday. I missed that trip. Dad couldn't understand why my husband and I didn't want to tour multiple cities, sites, and battlefields with infant twins in tow.

Now, in the church, Sid choked backed tears as he talked about that trip. My mother sat quietly, dazed, with my sister holding her hand. I was not sure she knew my father had died. From this weekend on, Sid and Nancy, who up to this point had lived in California, would care for my mother in her own home.

Reverend Wallace led the congregation in "The Last Journey." This ancient and important hymn was sung to accompany the bodies of Scottish kings to the island of Iona for burial. An organist could not be found for the ceremony, and no one in the church besides Reverend Wallace knew the melody. Still, I found the choice to be quite meaningful; Dad had been the leader of our clan.

As we made our way back outside, the bagpipers' "Amazing Grace" sustained us as we journeyed past the parish's cremation garden where Dad would, in time, be buried.

AT THE MEMORIAL reception, my parents' patio overflowed with the bouquets sent for the wedding, mingling with those sent for the memorial, all accompanied by the enormous arrangements of white roses that came home with us from the church. The fragrance of hundreds of roses and carnations hung in the humid air. Sid and Nancy donated the sandwiches they had ordered for the wedding luncheon, and the bottom layer of their wedding cake, saving the smaller top layers, with the tiny figures of a bride and groom, to serve the following day. During a time that felt strangely dreamlike, seeing that cake out of context struck me as the most surreal detail of all. There were also, oddly, electrical problems that suddenly came about. The overhead lights in my parents' kitchen kept flickering. Sparks flew out of the fuse box in the basement.

The evening passed quickly in the flurry of hugs, kisses, and conversations. Exhausted, I fell into bed at my friend's house. Just hours later, I walked back to my parents' house, where Reverend Wallace came to marry Sid and Nancy on the shaded lawn. Death and a new beginning merged into one, as seamlessly as day had followed the night. Someone had put a bow tie around the neck of the garden statue of Cupid. And there was my seventeen-year-old nephew, Nick, wearing my father's tuxedo. Nick had his arm around my mother; how kindly and maturely he behaved. My niece Alice played the cello.

The wedding was smaller and more intimate than the memorial. In the assemblage of those on folding chairs, I sat with my aunt Mary Jane Gable, my father's only sibling, and held her hand. A recent widow, she had lost her older son, my cousin John, to lung cancer just three months before my father's passing. The inner strength of this dear lady was extraordinary. And similarly, I felt absolutely in awe of her younger son, my cousin Patrick. Somehow, on this sad occasion, nearly back-to-back with another, he found the wherewithal to tell family jokes as we waited for the ceremony to begin.

Standing in front of the garden's lush greenery, Reverend Wallace took his place facing the guests. Sid entered the clearing wearing our Kirkpatrick family tartan kilt. Following her two daughters dressed in summer pink, Nancy, the lovely bride in white, joined my brother to begin their new life together.

I felt so proud of them. Individually strong, they made a mature and loving couple. The love that had carried them through this weekend would carry them through anything. They already knew that what comes to us in life may not always match what we had planned, but we can find our way by focusing on what matters.

Many emotions from the past two days rose in me. I tried not to cry once the ceremony began, but I couldn't help it. I sobbed. Sorrow. Grief. Love. Yearning. *Dad should be here*, I kept thinking.

Reverend Wallace told the story of the wedding at Cana. The miraculous love that blessed that wedding would bless this one as well. As my teary-eyed gaze turned to Sid that bright day, I beheld my father, in shimmering spirit form, standing behind Sid, and beheld my cousin John's spirit next to Patrick. Sid later confirmed that he'd felt my father's hand on his shoulder throughout the service. Dad's sister, Aunt Mary Jane, also said she'd felt my father's and John's presence near her.

Our father had come to the wedding, after all. And our family would draw strength from the amazing grace that would carry us all on the journey ahead.

Sid and Nancy at their wedding.

Dale and Audrey in Scotland.

PANDEMIC LIFE

Amy has been an emergency-room physician in Idaho for twenty-six years.

WRITE WHAT YOU KNOW

by Amy Baruch

I CAN ATTEST to knowing "tired." I've just come off a twenty-four-hour Emergency Department (ED) shift at the height of a COVID wave, having only slept thirty minutes. The oncoming physician, refreshed from a night's sleep and shower, looks and smells so much better than me. But I am now the one to be envied. I get to go home.

Before I leave, we do a quick deep dive, "How's family? Any good books?" I am always looking for a good Audible for my hour drive home. At sign out, we discuss several patients that await transfer to the main hospital in Boise. We are a freestanding emergency department. The closest hospitals are at capacity and our EMS crews are overwhelmed. All of our boarded patients either have COVID, or another diagnosis and tested positive on admission. "COVID-plus." Thankfully, none of my COVID patients waiting for beds required intubation. That typically happens later in their hospital stay.

I remove my mask long enough to caffeine up on the remnants from my large YETI mug. I toss it into my large cooler with the glass "Tupperware" that contained twenty-four hours of homemade sustenance. I sling the cooler and my oversized workbag over each shoulder. I thank the overnight crew and wish the new arrivals a good shift. As I pass through the ED entrance doors, I finally remove my mask. The cold is a refreshing shock to my face; and the odor from the nearby onion processing plant is so powerful, it could overcome a COVID-induced loss of smell.

I escape to my car and sit quietly for a few moments, relieved to be in complete silence. I start the car, and my Audible book, *The Lincoln Highway*, resumes where it left off, nearing its conclusion. On my ride home, I learn that Emmett leaves Duchess in a leaking boat with no oars and his fifty-thousand dollars in cash. I'm not sure how to feel. Does Duchess deserve to die just because he did so many terrible things?

The rush-hour traffic steadily worsens as I head into Boise, and my mind shifts. I feel a wave of increased fatigue. I do bellows breaths, a yoga technique, to sharpen my attention. I think of Indigo, my cat waiting for me at the top of stairs, to be fed. I will enter the house through the garage and laundry room, shed my layers of clothes, scrubs, compression hose, fleece-lined vest, and load them directly into the washing machine to run on "hot." Then, I will make my version of a penicillin: hot ginger tea, a fresh squeeze of lemon, honey enough to cover the bottom of the mug, and a splash of whisky. Finally, I will run from the backdoor to the outdoor hot tub, my mug in hand, into the 104-degree water. I will use this time to meditate, clear my head from the last twenty-four hours. But first I go on rewind.

Room 7, IG: Fourteen-year-old, observation for alcohol intoxication, level three times above the legal limit. His parents spoon on an adjacent stretcher.

Room 7, LD: An elderly female with a history of prior TIAs (transient ischemic attacks), after too many sleeping pills, woke up with numbness in her right hand, slowly improving. A code stroke is called, but a detailed history reveals that the numbness was only in the distribution of her thumb, index, and middle fingers, classic for acute carpal tunnel, and symptoms reproduced with Phalen's maneuver. She does not get a stroke workup. What if I made a wrong diagnosis? A potential misjudgment could be catastrophic.

Room 4, RR: A seventy-five-year-old male with vomiting and diarrhea for two days, presents profoundly dehydrated. He requires several liters of IV fluids. He is COVID positive. He has not completed the IV fluids, but decides he is ready to leave and attempts to walk out, still attached to the IV pole and pump. His mask is dangling from one ear as he parades down the main hallway.

Room 6, JC: A middle-age male, falls fifteen feet. The ladder he was climbing slipped, with his body still attached, impacting his left knee. His patella is fractured, and surgery is now needed. To support his family, he must be able to work, but this will not be possible.

Room 7, PB: A forty-four-year-old woman brought in by her husband, following a head injury. Her elementary school-aged son is sitting on an adjacent chair, playing on an electronic device, unfazed. Nurses are fretting because the woman is highly agitated. When I walk into the room, it is immediately apparent that she is high on methamphetamine or another stimulant. She denies use repeatedly, until I tell her that I, and the rest of my staff, are really worried about her. Her board of pharmacy suggests that narcotics are prescribed to her regularly, sixty tabs of hydrocodone every two weeks. I am angry not at her, but rather at her doctor.

Room 3, DS: A sixty-plus-year-old female rancher who slipped while doctoring her calves. She likely tore her ACL, a finding that cannot be seen on plain X-rays; the history of rapid swelling suggests the diagnosis. She cannot walk on her right leg due to pain. She has too many cattle to count. How will she manage with so many responsibilities on her ranch?

Room 7, AO: A twenty-six-year-old female with an underlying genetic disease, which caused her kidneys to fail. The day she was supposed to be placed on peritoneal dialysis, she received a kidney transplant. She takes three medications to prevent rejection, causing her to be immunocompromised. She has COVID pneumonia. Fortunately, her oxygen saturation is good. I wake up her nephrologist at two in the morning to help coordinate close follow-up care.

Room 9, MS: A seventy-year-old female with chest pain since sustaining a fall a week prior. She is tearful, reporting severe pain, and answers equivocally to questions regarding thoughts of self-harm. She lives alone. Dave, our star social worker, sits with her and provides her with options for home healthcare and assisted living. After ruling out a rib fracture and pneumonia, and providing Tylenol and a lidocaine patch for pain, she reports that her pain really isn't that bad, and she wants to go home.

Room 11, FR: A thirty-five-year-old, non-English-speaking male with acute anaphylaxis. His body is covered in an urticaria rash. He feels his throat closing and reports difficulty breathing. I am grateful for my ease with medical Spanish. He receives life-saving epinephrine, in addition to other medications, to prevent him from relapsing. He has a low-grade fever and tests positive for COVID.

Room 12, AR: A seventeen-year-old female whose pelvic pain is only eclipsed by her histrionics. I even see an eye roll from her mother. She is on day three of her menses, and she has bacterial vaginosis after an initial workup. She continues to report severe pain after being well-medicated. While we typically have ultrasound available during the day, we don't today because our one ultrasound technician is out sick with COVID. I am compelled to order a CT scan because of her intractable pain. Am I missing atypical appendicitis? The scan is normal. At discharge, only the mother expresses gratitude.

Room 6, NC: A sixty-one-year-old obese male with acute memory loss and markedly elevated systolic blood pressures, in the 230-250 range. He neglected to take his blood pressure medications this week due to field work. He completely normalizes with adequate blood pressure control.

Room 7, SR: A forty-seven-year-old female, morbidly obese and diabetic, with severe epigastric pain for several days. Her history suggests gallbladder disease. Again, ultrasound is not available. The CT scan demonstrates cholecystitis. She is admitted for antibiotics and surgery, without which she would likely become septic.

Room 4, NH: A fifty-nine-year-old female smoker, who looks much older than her stated years, with a COPD exacerbation. She is COVID positive but has no findings of pneumonia. Even with her usual supplemental oxygen, she cannot maintain her saturations above 75 percent. She stabilizes on high flow oxygen and must be admitted to the hospital.

Room 2, SB: A thirty-three-year-old female with cerebral palsy and seizure disorder who aspirated during a nighttime seizure. I am fortunately able to treat her as an outpatient with the help of her primary provider, who keeps his cell phone on for patient calls even when he is not on call.

Room 3, KW: Seventeen-year-old-old male brought in by parents, so "ill" he declines to speak on his own behalf. He has COVID symptoms. No over-the-counter medications were taken at home for symptoms. He does not have COVID. He has influenza and strep pharyngitis. Doses of ibuprofen and Tylenol bring him back to life.

Room 6, AC: An eighteen-year-old with severe left flank pain. His history suggests a stone, but his exam suggests an inflammatory process, with guarding. CT demonstrates a recently passed stone and an infected kidney. He is also COVID positive.

Room 5, DH: A forty-five-year-old with COVID symptoms and shortness of breath. She is COVID positive but does not have pneumonia and oxygen saturation is normal. She and her husband thought that this strain of COVID was "not supposed to be so bad." I explained that this strain is less likely to land you in the ICU or result in death.

Room 6, CT: Forty-year-old with a history of sickle cell disease, here for his weekly visit for "sickle cell crisis," without an established primary provider. He had been in the ED so many times, I was surprised I had not met him previously. According to old records, he had been repeatedly given IV narcotics and sent home with a prescription for hydrocodone. He had a generous board of pharmacy. His lab work does not support sickle cell crisis. He and his girlfriend make me uneasy. Real disease or drug-seeking?

Room 9 KS: A thirty-three-year-old male with groin pain. He had a hernia repair a few months prior and had attempted to lift a four-wheeler, feeling an instant pain in his groin. I suspect a groin strain given a normal exam. He insists on CT imaging; there is no recurrent hernia. A low-grade fever prompts COVID testing, and he is positive. When I tell him the result of the COVID test, his wife lectures me about COVID being a fake illness. I politely inform her that it is not a fake illness, and that I had treated many people during this shift for COVID who were very ill. I also let her know that there are many medical providers risking their own health to take care of these patients. I leave the room for the RN to discharge them home. I am a different kind of tired at this point.

I SAW SOMEWHERE between thirty and forty patients in this twenty-four-hour shift, mostly with COVID, but also COVID-like illness, broken fingers and ankles, back pain, dizziness, fatigue, chest pain, abdominal pain, constipation, kidney stones, and bloody diarrhea.

At home, I almost fall asleep in the hot tub, but startle awake. I wrap myself in a thick robe and make my way to the kitchen. I refresh a piece of homemade focaccia bread in the toaster oven, and smear on marinated goat cheese. I sit at the kitchen island, sipping my adulterated tea and eat. Indigo follows me everywhere. She hugs the leg of my stool and talks to me. I climb the stairs to my bedroom, and she follows. I remove all the decorative pillows, peel away the bedspread, and get in.

CALIFORNIA DREAMIN':
Playlist for a Pandemic

by Rhonda Hunt-Del Bene

FRIDAY. JANUARY 15, 2021. Somewhere on Pacific Coast Highway (PCH) in South Orange County, heading home. The Santa Ana winds blow westward from the Palm Springs desert, raising the coastal winter temperature to 81 degrees. Convertible top is down. Santana's "Smooth" blasts from the radio. In his throaty voice, Rob Thomas sings about feeling the heat of being inches from the noonday sun. The sun perches over the Pacific Ocean. From here, it seems to be about seven inches from dropping into the Ocean of Peace.

My fingers tap on the steering wheel, keeping time with the beat of the music. After the violence of the insurrection at our nation's capital just nine days ago, and a year in lockdown because of the COVID pandemic, for just one moment, all seems right with the world. I breathe in the luxury of this gifted moment and smile.

At home, it is still warm, so my husband and I move the *aperitivi*[12] to the *giardino*[13]. In Italy, any place where one grows plants is called a *giardino,* hence the patio has become known as *il giardino di Enzo,* my husband's garden.

He has transformed a once-bland patio into a veritable *paradiso.* He covered the concrete slab with rough-cut Italian marble tiles, blue with white veins running throughout. He replaced the vanilla-white fence with poplar panels, finished in a clear-coat to bring out its elegant natural grain, and installed them horizontally, shiplap style. He then planted drought-resistant succulents plus milkweed and salvia, in hand-crafted egg-pot planters from Marseilles, to attract butterflies. He even imported large pieces of petrified wood from our Arizona ranch and placed them among the plants.

---

12 In Italian, appetizers served prior to dinner.
13 Garden, pronounced *jar•deeno.*

Il giardino is secluded, quiet, with nary a neighbor in sight. It backs up to a gently rising hill covered with pines, eucalyptus, and pepper trees. Mexican honeysuckle shrubs march uphill, festooned with perennial bright orange blooms that attract endless numbers of hummingbirds, season after season. This hill has become an extension of *il giardino.* The back side of the hill drops down into Chaparossa Canyon, a conservation area wisely preserved by the city and home to our occasional visitor, the coyote.

TONIGHT, THE PLAYLIST for *aperitivi in giardino* begins with Sinatra. Martinis flow. "A whisper of vermouth in mine, please." The sliding doors remain open as we move effortlessly in a circle from kitchen to *giardino* to living room and back again. We stop to dance a few steps of an improvised waltz, twirling on the blue marble to "You Make Me Feel So Young." Sinatra is the perfect backdrop for martinis and dancing.

Early in the pandemic, we vowed not to cave to the hysteria of hoarding toilet paper and canned goods. Fresh foods were plentiful and since I could no longer travel or study at the university, I finally learned how to cook. We were adamant not to gain the "COVID-19-pounds" that our friends were complaining about, so I dusted off the *South Beach Diet* book and adapted the menus to gourmet-style meals, some of which rivaled dishes served by my friend Drew, a French chef who studied under Paul Bocuse and André Doré in France, including *poulet au porto* or *en papillote* [baked in parchment] and *filet en croute.* I substituted mashed potatoes with South Beach's "faux" potatoes made from cauliflower.

We decided that one way to relieve the stress and isolation of the pandemic would be to survive it in style, so meals became an "occasion." We served on our finest wedding china or plates from Italy. I shopped for champagne on sale, and we poured all libations into stemware typically reserved for guests.

Later that evening, after *aperitivi,* I served the filet mignon on hand-painted plates from Tuscany, and Enzo poured the wine into vintage glasses. Remembering my drive along PCH earlier, I switch the music to my "California Dreamin'" playlist, which starts with "California Gurls" by Snoop Dogg and Katy Perry singing about martinis and weenies and sex on the beach—although nowadays it is more commonly referred to as "cake by the ocean." When they get to the part about California girls wearing bikini tops and "Daisy Dukes," we share a laugh as we recall our

Florentine professor of Italian, Dario. Enzo and I had studied there in 2016. One day in class, we played this updated version of the Beach Boys's classic for Dario. Intrigued, but a little confused, he asked in his inimitable accent, "What are Daisy Dukes?" I explained the cut-off jeans that go in and out of fashion here from time to time.

The playlist continues with two versions of "California Dreamin'," the original by the Mamas & the Papas from 1965, followed by José Feliciano's haunting rendition, infused with a sense of melancholy. I love California.

Life is good.

MY THOUGHTS RETURN to the pandemic. *Il giardino* has become an important focal point in this viral season, where we are all challenged to be our own safe place—*our own Savior*. Now it is even more of a sanctuary. In 2020, we celebrated birthdays and our thirtieth wedding anniversary, just the two of us. We are cognizant of how fortunate we are that our lives were not drastically affected. We have acquaintances who lost their jobs, their homes, and even their lives to COVID. Reverently, we express our gratitude and send blessings of love and support to all those less fortunate.

AROUND MIDNIGHT THE only sound is the forlorn hooting of an owl in a eucalyptus tree somewhere on the hill. *Il giardino* settles into silence. A chill creeps into the air, crawling up the canyon from the Ocean of Peace. Its repetitive waves move quietly, rhythmically, somewhere below us. We are just four hundred feet above sea level. Enzo lights the patio heaters for me, then leaves for bed. Replacing my wine, I drink a cup of hot Chamomile tea in a Limoges café-au-lait cup with saucer, acquired at Saint-Paul-de-Vence when we vacationed in the Provence region of France ten years ago.

I sip the tea, then lean back and sigh. I half expect a coyote to lope by.

The Santa Ana winds have cleared the clouds from the night sky. A new moon appears, symbolic of a second chance being gifted to us. A new administration will be inaugurated in five days. Under my breath, I whisper a prayer, "May it usher in peace and unity, please dear God." We can always hope—without the prospect of hope, we are lost.

I play one final song, will.i.am's, "It's a New Day."

DEAR MAMA

by Kathleen M. Rodgers

It's not fair
that a woman your age
a child who remembers rationing
and blackout shades at night
should have to live out your golden years
holed up in a house where you raised your kids.
It's not fair that you had to ration toilet paper
while a madman in office sits on his "royal" throne
thumbing his smart phone with riddles and lies
as a pandemic rages across our country like storm troopers
threatening to invade and kill every person
regardless of age, gender, race, religion, or economic status.
You've gone months without seeing your family and friends;
each time you walk to the mailbox or head to the store
you strap on a mask to cover your face
like a shield trying to block an invisible enemy.
While you wait for a vaccine
you read and watch news and talk on the phone
or scroll through Facebook biding your time.
You pray that you can survive the ruthlessness
from a man who's supposed to protect you and your fellow Americans.
At eighty-four,
you've survived tragedies and traumas
and always spring back.
I hope the country you served
as a civilian working for the military
can spring back from the cruel policies of a sociopath and his enablers
threatening to dismantle our democracy.

I wish for a day when you can pull down your nightshades
trusting you'll wake up
to another sunrise
and the chance to travel again
to live out your golden years
in freedom.

For my mother, Patricia Lamb Doran
November 10, 2020

OBSTRUCTED VIEW

by Andrea Simon

IN MY EIGHT-by-ten-foot study, my computer sits on a long oak desk built against the wall, abutting the picture window directly facing Riverside Park and beyond the Hudson River and New Jersey shoreline. From my black-mesh swivel chair, my view to the outdoors is shrouded by the objects on my desk: a smashed yellow mylar balloon with a smiley face ribboned to a clear glass vase jammed with a fall array of burnt-orange lilies and drooping yellow roses amongst pink sprays of alstroemeria; a smaller vase of yellow and red chrysanthemums; and a short, thin vase with one rich dark crimson peony and a tall stalk of white fluffy pampas grass whose thin strands stick out as if blasted by static electricity. The week-old bouquets are get-well gifts from my beloved writing group and my dear cousins to mark my latest cancer surgery. The room smells of earth, a heady mix of wet sod mixed with the sulfuric odor of rotten eggs. I will give the withering blooms a few more days before I throw them out. Still cheered by the imagined faces behind them, hugging me in a riot of color, I am not ready to celebrate my recent escape from medical disaster and face my uncertain future.

Though smaller than the vases, the silky peony occupies my attention. My daughter, Zoe, brought it from her local florist in Brooklyn, who specializes in artful arrangements. At first glance, it looks like a small magenta cabbage head, a fistful of curved velvety leaves. I shine my overhead spotlight on the flower and the deep purple shows off its hues; the bottom double leaves are a lighter fuchsia, variegated in its decaying stages. The tightly wound center reminds me of the fake carnation tissues we used to make as children, so fluffy and layered. I didn't know that peonies came in such a color; I hope it wasn't sprayed like the unearthly turquoise at the flower stall of my local Korean market.

I don't want to focus solely on these flowers. They are temporary distractions. Many other items occupy more permanent places on my desk, and I don't have to leave my chair to reach them: my Lenovo PC, a huge black Brother printer, my landline phone, computer speakers, router, stapler, pen cups, and green two-pound weights gathering dust now holding down bills.

Facing the chair, underneath the desk, a pull-out drawer, originally designed for a keyboard, now holds stray tissue papers, greeting cards, wrapping paper, nettings, old painting cutouts—a mishmash of collage material that lays unsorted like the groundcover of a blistery fall day. The desk's drawers keep ephemera, from old Social Security cards to reams of address labels. The bottom drawer has financial statements and receipts for the past seven years. Atop the printer is a stack of bestselling novels for reminders. Unlike the time an interviewer asked me what books were on my bedside table and I couldn't remember one, now I wouldn't sound like Ralph Kramden's tongue-tied diatribe. Underneath a middle section, there is a scanner, various manilla files, and a large cardboard carton filled with my unpublished manuscripts and research on the 1960s for my latest novel.

I don't have to go far from my desk. My life lays before me, held up by this slab of oak. If I attend art class or my writing groups, I turn on Zoom, where I can mute my voice or cancel my image at will.

Above my eye level, my wall calendar looms, displaying the abstract paintings that change with each month. In small script and black magic marker, I noted my appointments and important birthdays. In red ink, below each month, I indicated the last dates of medical procedures and surgeries. Though I can't forget these, I need reminders. Whenever I notice a red mark, my heartbeat automatically intensifies, and I turn the page.

I STAND AND move the flowers from my view. What do I see? The whitened branches of sycamores intertwine with oaks and maples, revealing slate glimpses of the Hudson. I look down at the small park where I used to take our springer spaniel, Abby, for daily walks. There were times, especially during winter ice storms, still smarting from the wind tunnel of Riverside Drive, when I unabashedly yelled at her to "pee for God's sake."

This park ends with another Riverside Drive and then the cobblestone pedestrian walkway with sloped entrances to the lower park level. In these days of illness and COVID, when I am weakened or afraid of contagion, I don't have to go there. Just by looking out the window, I trace the mile route from my former thrice-weekly walks. I don't have to stop at the café across from the dog walk and admire the sexual canine foreplay. I don't have to cross 96th Street and enter the blossom tree path toward the People's Park and watch neighbors weed their little parcels. I don't have to detour down the steep slope to the furthest park area by the Hudson, with its northern views of the George Washington Bridge. I don't have to remember my frail eighty-three-year-old mother who couldn't make it up that hill during the parade of tall ships at 2000 Operation Sail and collapsed on a bench to gather her strength. I live in my memories, here at my desk.

When Zoom calls, I greet my friends and relatives as if they are coming through my front door. They don't see what I see; they have a backward view of my red velour couch and pink flower kimono wall hanging. From my peripheral vision, I can still catch the sunlight along New Jersey's shoreline like a swash of iridescent yellow paint. I rearrange my vases. Even the decaying and peeling flowers are full enough to obscure my view.

MORE ABOUT US

Amy Baruch writes from Boise, Idaho. She was born in Brooklyn, grew up in the suburbs of Long Island, and attended college at Bryn Mawr. The entirety of her medical training was at SUNY Stony Brook. Seduced by the big skies, mountains, and rivers of Idaho, she has been practicing emergency medicine in Boise for twenty-six years. She will remain in her house on Villa Norte Street, with its too many stairs and a beautiful view of the Boise foothills, for as long as her heart and legs will allow. The proud mother of Michelle, Amy is grateful for her many wonderful friends, especially the Lady Bunch, and her family who remains on the East Coast.

Stephanie Cowell has been an opera singer, balladeer, and founder of Strawberry Opera and other arts venues, including a Renaissance festival and an outdoor music and dance series in New York City. She is the author of *Nicholas Cooke: Actor, Soldier, Physician, Priest*; *The Physician of London*; *The Players: A Novel of the Young Shakespeare*; *Marrying Mozart*; *Claude & Camille: A Novel of Monet*; and *A Boy in the Rain*. Forthcoming September 2025: *The Man in the Stone Cottage*, a story of the Brontë sisters. Her work has been translated into nine languages and adapted into an opera. Stephanie is the recipient of an American Book Award. She lives in New York City and has two grown sons and grandchildren. She loves opera and early music, Europe, theater (and of course, Shakespeare), mountains, the sea, and especially being with friends.

Linda Aronovsky Cox grew up in a military family, living all over the world until graduating from high school in Madrid, Spain. She received a bachelor's degree in psychology and a master's degree in communications from Ohio University in Athens, Ohio, and has lived in Austin, Texas, for more than forty years, where she raised her now-grown daughter. Linda spent her career in public information, program development, and marketing communications in a wide range of fields in the government sector. After a lifetime of writing for organizations, when she retired several years ago, she refocused her creative energies on memoir—personal stories of the myriad life challenges she has faced—and has begun researching and writing the story of her mother who escaped Belgium as a child during the Holocaust. For the past thirty-five years, Linda has also owned and operated a home-based, used, rare, and out-of-print book business, Saddlebag Books.

Karen Finch is a multidisciplinary arts practitioner. A classically trained alto, she spent thirty years singing opera, jazz classics, and Jewish liturgical music professionally. She holds a degree in visual art, and a master's in art history and curatorial studies. Her artwork is held in numerous public and private collections across Australia and internationally. Karen's writing stems from her academic studies and began with coverage of the Australian arts and crafts scene, and also two chapters in the 2010 work, *It's No Secret: Real Men Wear Aprons*, the first major book about Freemasonry in Australia. She works as a ghostwriter for businesses, and more recently has been exploring creative nonfiction and memoir. Born in Sydney, Australia, she has moved around the country, and is now settled in Melbourne, Victoria, with her partner and two Siamese cats.

Jane Mylum Gardner was raised in Wilson, North Carolina, and moved to New York City in 1969, where she lived for thirty-three years. During that time, Jane pursued an independent study of artists and their creative processes. After attending a silent writer's retreat with famed author Madeleine L'Engle, Jane joined an offshoot group in 1989. Three of these writers, Andrea, Katherine, and Stephanie, are now part of the Lady Bunch group. Jane's book, *Henry Moore: From Bones and Stones to Sketches and Sculptures,* was published in 1993 by Four Winds Press and made the coveted Blue Ribbons Children's picture books list. After Madeleine's passing, Jane and others wrote memorial essays published in a book, *A Circle of Friends*, edited by Katherine Kirkpatrick. Following 9/11/01, Jane returned to her hometown in 2002, and taught elementary- and middle-school art. During COVID, Jane was "tremendously nourished" by her writing groups and art classes, which met via Zoom. "Letting go of some of those old critical voices has given me a sense of freedom and allows me to value my truths as I see and experience them."

Rhonda Hunt-Del Bene is a devoted Southern California resident, but with an international soul. She lives with her husband, Paul, an Italian American with dual citizenship. She was raised on a ranch in northern Arizona. She studied French at Brigham Young University, as well as in Paris, France, at the Alliance Française. She had a long career in shopping center development in California and Las Vegas. Recently, she reignited her passion for language studies, this time for Italian. She studied at CSU-Long Beach, Florence University of the Arts in Florence, Italy, and Saddleback College. In 2023, she graduated with degrees in Italian, political science, and fine arts & humanities. She has grown deep roots in Italy and will soon have dual citizenship. She plans to live there part time and teach English as a foreign language.

Katherine Kirkpatrick grew up in Stony Brook, New York, and now lives in Seattle with her husband and their two children. She is the author of nine books, both fiction and nonfiction, including *The Snow Baby*, a *Booklist* Editors' Choice and recipient of the James Madison Award Honor; and *Mysterious Bones*, awarded the Golden Kite Honor, a *School Library Journal* Best Book of the Year, and a Children's Book Council/ National Science Teachers Association Notable Trade Book. Her most recent title, *The Art of William Sidney Mount: Long Island People of Color on Canvas*, coauthored with Vivian Nicholson-Mueller, features the true-life stories of the anonymous Black and multiracial models who posed for the acclaimed nineteenth-century artist. A forthcoming book, *To Chase the Glowing Hours: A Novel of Egypt and Highclere*, will be published by Regal House in 2025. Katherine studied English and art history at Smith College and is a painter, as well as a writer. Her knowledge and enthusiasm for literature, art, history, and archaeology were instilled in her by her late mother, Audrey Kirkpatrick.

Kathleen M. Rodgers is a novelist whose work has appeared in *Family Circle Magazine*, *Military Times*, and in several anthologies. A professional writer for over forty-five years, her novels have garnered many awards and favorable reviews. She's been featured in *USA Today*, *The Associated Press*, and *Military Times*. A native of Clovis, New Mexico, Kathleen's latest novel, *The Flying Cutterbucks*, is the New Mexico Press Women 2022 Zia Book Award First Runner-Up and a 2021 WILLA Literary Award Finalist in Contemporary Fiction from Women Writing the West. She and her husband, Tom, a retired USAF fighter pilot/commercial airline pilot, live in a suburb of North Texas with two rescue dogs. After raising two sons, she became a grandmother and has recently completed her fifth novel. Kathleen often says, "I am always the daughter trying to write my way home."

Andrea Simon is a published author of three diverse, award-winning books: *Bashert: A Granddaughter's Holocaust Quest*, a memoir/history, republished in paperback, and topping the list for the 2021 Book Authority's "Best Holocaust Biography Books of All Time"; *Esfir Is Alive*, a historical novel, a 2016 INDIES Book of the Year Award Finalist and 2017 Moonbeam Children's Book Awards winner; and *Floating in the Neversink*, a novel-in-stories about growing up in the Catskills and Brooklyn in the 1950s, which won the 2020 New York Indie Author Project. As a native New Yorker, Andrea has a public-school education, from kindergarten to graduate school. She holds an MFA in Creative Writing from City College. A proud member of two writing groups, Andrea has also taught and mentored many a scribbler. The mother of a grown daughter, she lives in Manhattan with her husband.

ACKNOWLEDGMENTS

Unlike any single-author work, an anthology requires several levels of editorial and emotional assistance. Each author goes through a collaborative process as she selects a topic that relates to the book's overall theme. She then performs research, writing, and editing pertaining to her story, always keeping in mind how it fits into the whole. Often, the author works with the other contributors and the book's editor in fine-tuning her work. Along the way, we have personal "helpers," those who have not only assisted us in the nuts and bolts of creation, but who have provided necessary support and inspiration. As a group of contributors, we Lady Bunchers give them all a collective and heartfelt "thanks."

For this anthology, we also thank the Story Circle Network, the writing and educational organization that got us together. Its president and online course coordinator, Helen (Len) Leatherwood, has been a beacon of encouragement and wrote us a terrific review. We also greatly appreciate other pre-publication reviews from the talented and erudite Lene Andersen, Mary Caputi, Deborah Kalb, Ruth Pennebaker, and D.Z. Stone. Ms. Stone and E. Jean Zgutowicz also provided excellent and timely copy editing and proofreading assistance.

Our publisher, Bedazzled Ink, accepted our book wholeheartedly, and we are very grateful. Thanks to the expert team: owner and publisher, Claudia Wilde; managing editor and typesetter, C.A. Casey; and acquisitions editor and author liaison, Liz Gibson.

And we of the Lady Bunch thank all those who have believed in our writing over the years.

Printed in the USA
CPSIA information can be obtained
at www.ICGtesting.com
LVHW090407160324
774635LV00001B/156

9 781960 373434